SECRET

VENICE LAGOON

Debora Gusson and Riccardo Roiter Rigoni

JONGLEZ PUBLISHING

Travel guides

We have taken great pleasure in drawing up *Secre* *Venice Lagoon* and hope that through its guidanc you will, like us, continue to discover unusual, hidden o little-known aspects of the region.
Descriptions of certain places are accompanied by themati sections highlighting historical details or anecdotes as an ai to understanding the region in all its complexity.
Secret Venice Lagoon also draws attention to the multitude o details found in places that we may pass every day withou noticing. This is an invitation to look more closely at th urban landscape and, more generally, it is a means of seein our own region with the curiosity and attention that w often display while travelling elsewhere ...

Comments on this guide and its contents, as well a information on sites not mentioned, are welcome and wil help us to enrich future editions.

Don't hesitate to contact us:
Email: info@jonglezpublishing.com

Debora Gusson, born in Dolo on April 18, 1986, is a researcher and author dedicated to the analysis and promotion of the historical and cultural heritage of Venice and the Veneto region. A graduate of the Istituto d'Arte in Venice with a Master of Arts in pictorial ornamentation and a degree in cultural heritage conservation from Ca' Foscari University in Venice, she has developed her skills in the fields of historical research, iconography, and cultural anthropology. Her thesis on the fortifications of the Campo Trincerato in Mestre marked the beginning of her in-depth studies on the Venetian territory, leading her to extensive research and publication of articles. Her work focuses on historical anthropology, with a deep knowledge of the rural traditions of Veneto, the main festivities of the region, and the anthropological links between rituality and local history. Debora Gusson regularly contributes to specialist journals such as *Medioevo*, *Storia Veneta*, and *L'Esde - fascicoli di studi e cultura*, and has participated in numerous thematic conferences in various locations, focusing in particular on the lagoon islands and Venetian peculiarities. She has also put her skills as an independent researcher to use in video and multimedia productions as a consultant and has contributed to radio programs dedicated to Venetian culture and folklore. Among her main works, she is the author of the book *Venice from Above*, published internationally in October 2022 by Jonglez. Alongside her writing, she plays an active role in cultural promotion, for example through her participation in the jury for the Parfin Dolse cultural prize and her management, with Riccardo Roiter Rigoni, of the Facebook page Rii Interai, a reference for enthusiasts of Venetian culture and history. She wrote most of the texts for *Secret Venice Lagoon* and was also responsible for historical archive research and supervising the editing of the entire work.

Riccardo Roiter Rigoni, photographer and author, was born in Venice Lido in 1979. Professionally active since 2001, his work has resulted in photographic books such as *Venezia Sensation* (Granviale Editori, 2008), *Venezia momenti senza tempo* (Marcianum Press, 2012), *Il mare d'inverno esiste davvero* (Duck Edizioni, 2016) and *Venice from the skies* (Jonglez Publishing, 2022). He is also the author of the novel *Come la Luna alle porte dell'alba* (Duck Edizioni, 2019). He took the photographs for Il Gioco dell'oca città di Venezia (2018), the cover images for the catalog of the art exhibition 50 anni di Luna Nuova organized by Anna Caterina Bellati (2019), and the cover photos for the books *Marco, Patriarca amato da tutti* (CID Edizioni, 2015), *Com'è gialla Venezia* (Mazzanti Libri, 2021), and *Marco Cé fedeltà e profezia* (Marcianum Press, 2024). He has also been responsible for the photography in a number of books published by Filippi Editore, Edizioni CID, and Marcianum Press.
From 2003 to 2006, he documented the Landfall art center artistic happening conceived and directed by Swiss architect Antonio Rodriguez. His vision was chosen to represent institutional initiatives such as the official posters for the 44th (2018) and 47th (2023) VOGALONGA and the photographs for the Italian Post Office's Folder Filatelico Venezia (2018). Riccardo Roiter Rigoni is particularly known for his research and documentation on Venice and its lagoon in the field of aerial photography. He is behind artistic performances such as A Message of Light, the world's first photograph of a mask flying through the sky above Venice. In 2020, he designed and produced the aerial photograph *VENETIE MMXX, omaggio a Jacopo de Barbari*, which has become an image of civic value, used as the background for the City of Venice's website dedicated to the celebrations of the city's 1600th anniversary. This photograph was the starting point for the writing, in

collaboration with Debora Gusson, of the texts *1600 anni di Venezia un'idea di futuro* (*1600 years of Venice: an idea of the future*) and *Dall'immaginazione all'immagine* (From imagination to image). *Venezia tra cartografia e fotografia* (*1600 Years of Venice: An Idea for the Future and From Imagination to Image*), subsequently published in Atlantis, a geopolitical magazine. His works have been published in various newspapers, including Corriere della Sera, Il Gazzettino, La Nuova Venezia, and Bollettino, a magazine published by Casa Cipriani in New York. Since 2005, he has been collaborating with the weekly magazine Gente Veneta and, since 2021, he has been co-authoring the Facebook page Rii Interai with Debora Gusson, a reference in terms of historical and cultural dissemination about the region. He is the author of all the photographic documentation (unless otherwise stated) in *Secret Venice Lagoon* and has written some of the texts.

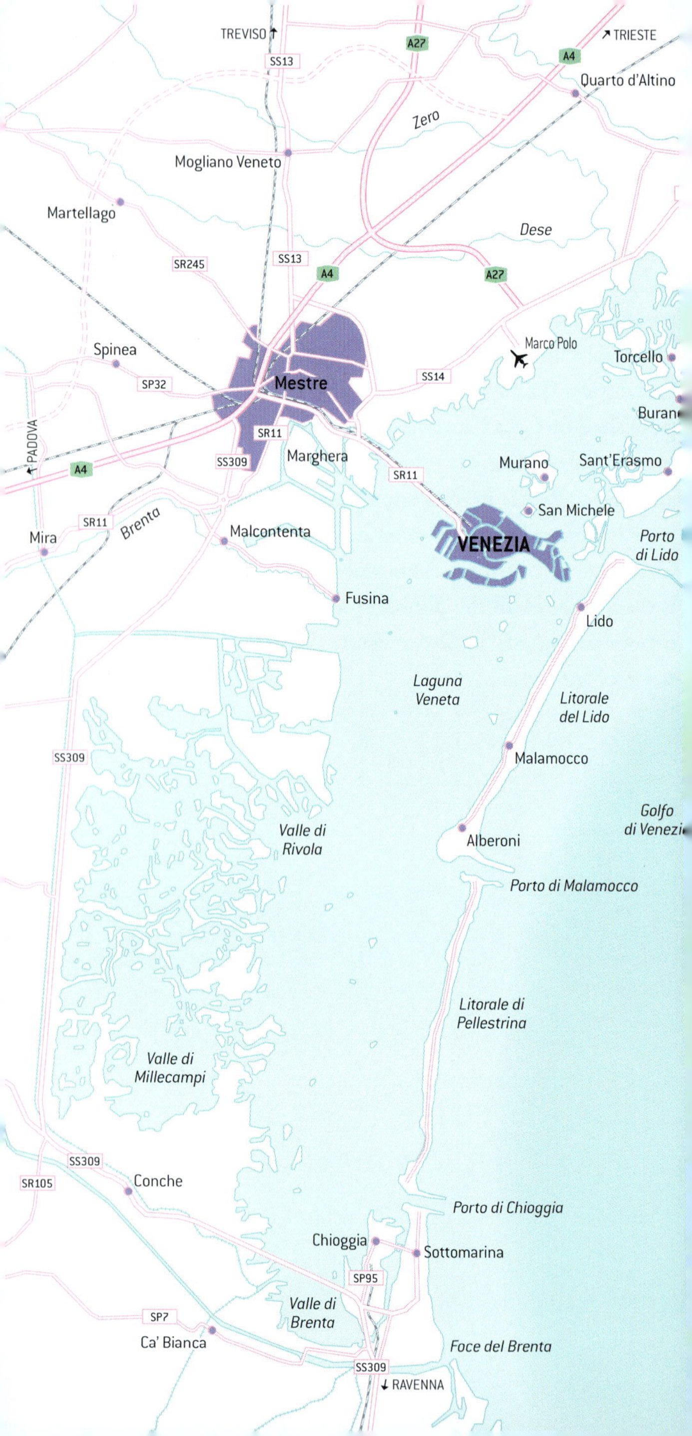
TREVISO
SS13
A27
A4
TRIESTE
Quarto d'Altino
Zero
Mogliano Veneto
Martellago
Dese
SR245
SS13
A4
A27
Spinea
Marco Polo
Torcello
SP32
Mestre
SS14
Burano
PADOVA
SR11
SS309
Marghera
Murano
Sant'Erasmo
A4
SR11
San Michele
SR11
Brenta
Malcontenta
VENEZIA
Porto di Lido
Mira
Fusina
Lido
Laguna Veneta
Litorale del Lido
SS309
Malamocco
Golfo di Venezia
Valle di Rivola
Alberoni
Porto di Malamocco
Litorale di Pellestrina
Valle di Millecampi
SS309
SR105
Conche
Porto di Chioggia
Chioggia
Sottomarina
SP95
Valle di Brenta
SP7
Ca' Bianca
Foce del Brenta
SS309
RAVENNA

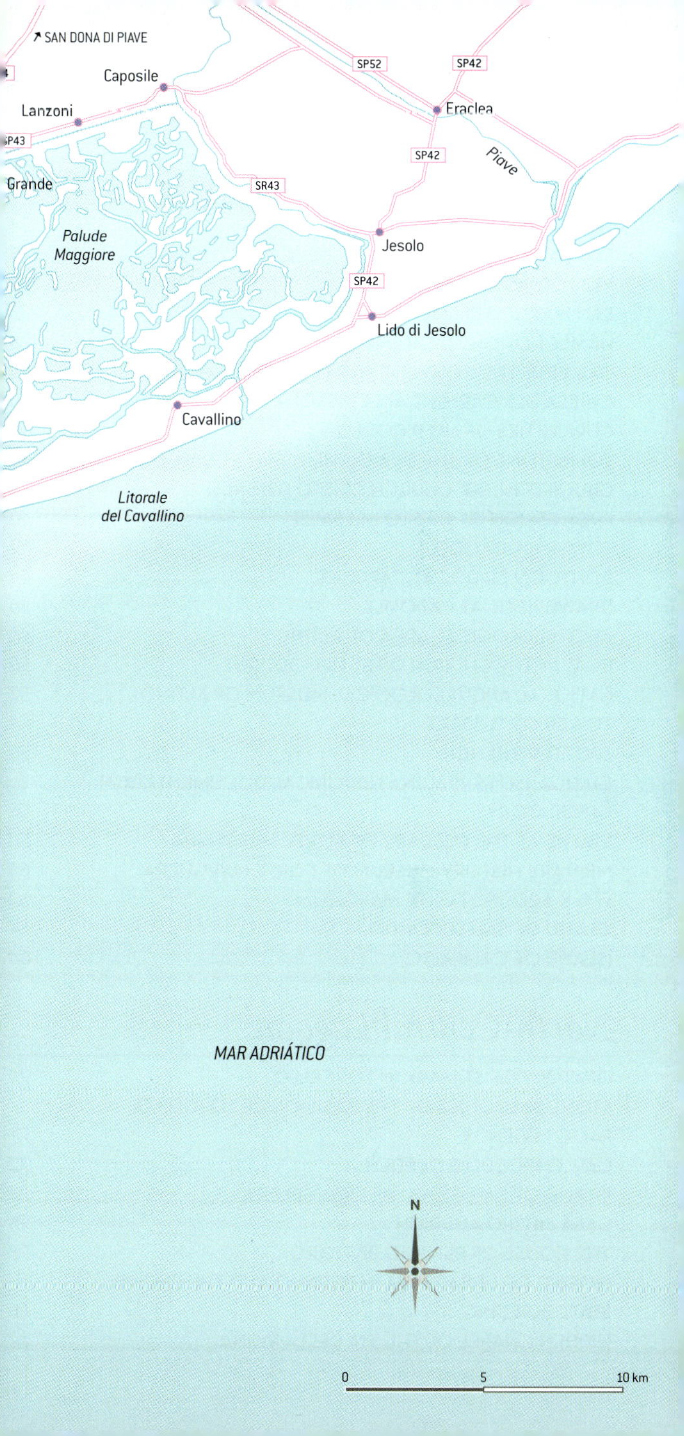

SAN DONA DI PIAVE
Caposile
Lanzoni
SP43
SP52
SP42
Eraclea
SP42
Piave
Grande
SR43
Palude Maggiore
Jesolo
SP42
Lido di Jesolo
Cavallino
Litorale del Cavallino
MAR ADRIÁTICO
N
0
5
10 km

CONTENTS

Northern Lagoon

North-Central Lagoon

Venice Lido

CONTENTS

Central Lagoon

Southern Lagoon

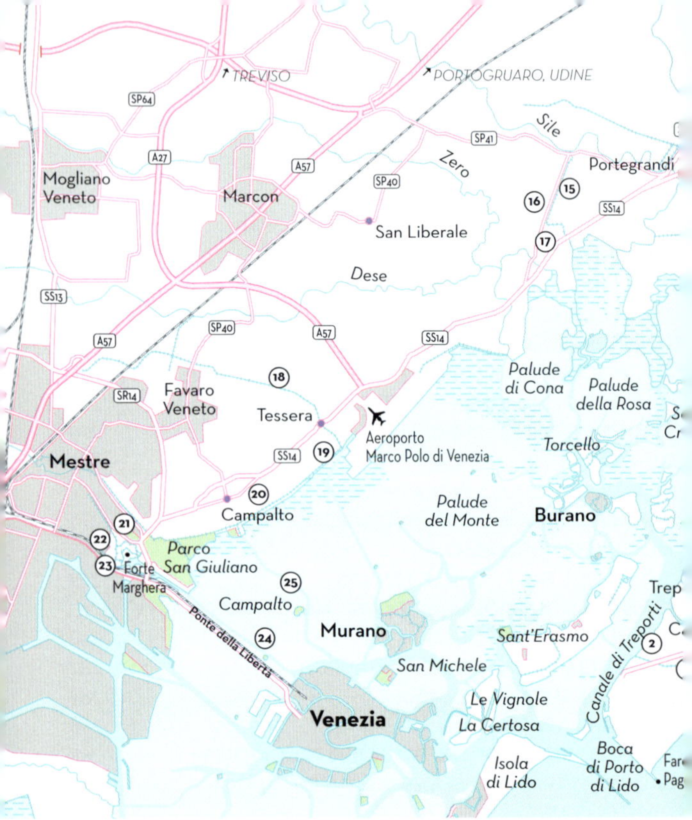

Northern Lagoon

SP47
SP43
SP52
SP47
Eraclea
Piave
glio del Sile
Santa Maria
di Piave
SP42
Valle
Doga
nale Cenesa
Sile
SP43
Jesolo
Valle
Grassabo
Valle
Dragojesolo
SP42
Palude
Maggiore
Valle
Cavallino
SP42
Lido di Jesolo
Lio Piccolo
Valle
Paleazza
Mesole
Ca' di Valle
SP42
Mare
Adriatico
N
0
5
10 km

THE AMALFI BATTERY

1

The most important coastal artillery battery in the Adriatic

Via Retrone, 2 – 30013 Ca' Savio (VE)
viadeiforti.it/it
Can only be visited from the outside

Construction of the Amalfi Battery began in September 1915 and was completed in May 1917. It constituted the most important coastal artillery in the Adriatic, capable of firing huge shells with a firing rate of one shot per minute and a range of almost 19 km.

Armed with a double-barrelled anti-aircraft gun, it made a great contribution to the control of the bridges over the Piave River and was ready to intervene in June 1918 during the Battle of Solstice.

The structure was dedicated to the memory of the fallen heroes of the cruiser Amalfi, which was sunk in the northern Adriatic Sea on 7

uly 1915 by a German submarine.

The event is commemorated by the motto on the entrance portal: *Ex imo fluctuum contra hostes resurgo* ('From the depths of the waves I e-emerge against the enemy').

The battery was part of a military complex comprised of 14 buildings, vith both the munitions depot and the main garrison quarters located at distance, connected to the battery by covered walkways, some of which ave now partially collapsed. Of significant technological importance, he site was visited by King Vittorio Emanuele III, as well as a Japanese lelegation and numerous groups of Allied officers. Following restoration nd safety works by the Veneto Region, the structure has been partially preserved, and the surrounding outdoor areas have been transformed into accessible green spaces equipped for picnics.

The site can be reached on foot, by bicycle or by car. While it can only be viewed from the outside, visitors can still enjoy the picturesque landscape in which it is set.

FORTE TREPORTI

Before 1882, the fort stood between the sea and the lagoon

Via Lungomare S. Felice, 96 – Punta Sabbioni (VE)
viadeiforti.it/it
Can only be visited from the outside

Right at the tip of the Cavallino coastline, built on the remain of an earlier French fortification, stands Forte Treporti – an important military structure also known as *Forte Vecchio* (Old Fort). It was constructed in 1845 during the second Austrian occupation to control the Punta Sabbioni port entrance and part of the lagoon.

It seems almost impossible today, but before 1882 – when the Punta Sabbioni breakwater was built – the fort stood directly between the sea and the lagoon, occupying an extremely strategic position.

Surrounded by a moat and equipped with a drawbridge, the fort underwent various changes over the years. New structures like telemetric towers were added and obsolete buildings demolished.

After World War II, it lost its military function and housed several families who looked after the structure, some living there until quite recently.

Later it became home to a rowing club and various cultural and sports associations. Since February 2022 it has belonged to the State Property Agency, which has put it up for sale.

Listed among FAI's *Luoghi del Cuore* (Places of the Heart – an initiative to identify and protect Italy's most cherished heritage sites), there's hope the interior will be restored and the fort added to the Via dei Forti heritage route. Even though you can only view it from outside, it's well worth visiting; this is a fascinating building in many ways.

VETTOR PISANI BATTERY

The most significant coastal defence battery

Via Vettor Pisani, 40
Cavallino-Treporti (VE)
viadeiforti.it
info@viadeiforti.it

In the early 1900s, to strengthen the defence of Venice against possib attacks from the sea, several coastal batteries, with respective telemetr towers, were built along the Cavallino coastline.

These towers were capable of thwarting naval fleets equipped wit increasingly modern weaponry.

By early 1913, there were as many as 37 forts and main batteri operational along the 'land front' and 'sea front', and a number support structures in various nearby locations.

Of these, the most significant today is certainly the Vettor Pisa Battery, built between 1909 and 1912. It is named after the Venetia commander who defeated the Genoese fleet in the War of Chioggia i 1380.

Consisting of a central section more than 80 metres long, two turre and two wings with terraces on which the telemetry and observatio installations were located, it was armed with six 280 mm howitzer which were decommissioned during World War II to house an ant aircraft post.

The battery was connected by rails to the barracks, the powder agazine and the small military port of Cà Vio, where materials from enice were sorted. This narrow-gauge railway is called Decauville, and as invented in the mid-19th century by the French company from hich it takes its name. It was very quick to lay and remove, even on rticularly uneven terrain, and thanks to this characteristic it was used uring both world wars. After being decommissioned, the structure oused a few civilian families for several years, and it was only in 1951 at the embankment protecting the side facing the sea was removed.

Recently restored by the Municipality of Cavallino-Treporti, it has oused the War Museum since 2017 and is the fulcrum of the 'Via ei Forti' (Route of the Forts) itinerary: a scattered museum with an inerary covering 13 km of coastline and around 200 fortifications cluding telemetry towers, batteries, bunkers, powder magazines, rracks and shelters.

The Vettor Pisani fort is also part of the Walk of Peace Project, hich promotes the conservation and enhancement of the historical eritage of World War I through an itinerary covering sites marked by e war, bringing them back to life through art and promoting, through membrance, the values of peace and fellowship between peoples.

Inside the museum is a work by artist Luigi Ballarin, *Knave of Hearts*, hich fits in well with the museum's exhibitions which include various eryday objects, medical tools and instruments, armaments and quipment.

SAN MARCO TELEMETRY TOWER

The coffee pot

Via delle Batterie – Cavallino-Treporti (VE)
Can only be visited from the outside

Among the many testimonies of military activities along the Cavallino-Treporti coastline are various telemetry towers. Most of ›em have been disused for years, none of them can be visited but are ›sible from the outside.

They served as sighting points from which, thanks to precision ›lescopes and rangefinders, potential targets were spotted. The firing ›ordinates were then promptly transmitted to the various battalions, ›hich directed the shots of their cannons based on this data.

The locals used to call telemetry towers 'traffic lights' because large, ›loured discs were once placed on top of them.

Some of these towers have deliberately anonymous shapes, but one has peculiar appearance: the San Marco telemetry tower which, due to its ›aracteristic shape, is called 'the coffee pot'.

The construction has a truncated conical shape with an upper platform ›riginally made of wood.

On the base, there is an engraving of a star alongside the year the ›ilding was constructed: 1915.

›EARBY

›ear the San Marco telemetry tower stands the former San Marco ›attery, built between 1909 and 1912. This impressive two-storey ›mplex originally housed two 305/50 cannons and two 76/40 anti-›rcraft guns.

›uring World War I, the battery played an active role in operations ›gainst the land front in the Grisolera-San Donà di Piave sector, ›articularly in June and October 1918. Remarkably, it emerged ›nscathed from both world wars. By early 1944, the battery was staffed ›y two officers and 30 soldiers.

›oday, the site is part of a tourist village. While the original structure ›as been adapted, its basic shape remains intact. The two domes have ›een replaced by a small swimming pool and a sweeping spiral staircase. ›he roof has been rebuilt, and various tourist amenities have been ›dded. The interior spaces now house businesses, including a bar and restaurant.

›he original entrance gate is still in place, and a small section of the ›acks once used to transport ammunition and supplies to the battery ›n still be seen.

The floating Nativity scenes in Cavallino – Treporti

Starting in spring, but especially in summer, the municipality of Cavallino-Treporti has a flood of tourists who choose to spend their holidays there or enjoy brief stays at the area's renowned campsites.

Visitors who venture to this region during the Christmas season, however, encounter a cherished local tradition that has evolved into a celebrated custom: the *presepi sull'acqua* (Nativity scenes on water).

The Nativity is depicted through installations set in the lagoon, just a few centimetres above the water's surface, creating a particularly enchanting natural setting.

One such scene can be admired in the heart of Cavallino, from the panoramic terrace at Piazza Santa Maria Elisabetta, and is managed by members of the local rowing association.

Another especially admired Nativity scene is located in the waters in front of the historic centre of Lio Piccolo. This display often incorporates elements that reflect the local environment.

The Lagoon Nativity is a Guinness World Record-breaking work, the only one of its kind, which winds its way along the Via Pordelio canal leading from Ca' Ballarin to Ca' Savio.

About 200 statues, or rather marine plywood figures, make up this Nativity scene created in collaboration with artist Francesco Orazio and a carpentry company from Jesolo.

It was first installed in 2023 to commemorate the 800th anniversary of Saint Francis of Assisi's first Nativity re-enactment in Greccio.

The supports holding the figures are driven into the seabed, where the water is only a few dozen centimetres deep, allowing the figures to emerge from the water.

The images remain in place throughout the display period.

The Three Wise Men, however, are initially positioned at a distance from the Nativity scene and are gradually moved closer as the Epiphany draws nearer and they reach the end of their journey.

The tradition of water-based Nativity scenes has spread to other parts of the Venetian Lagoon. Notable examples include those in Burano and Le Giare.

THE HAMLET OF SACCAGNANA ⑤

A magical atmosphere where time seems to stand still

Via del Prà
Cavallino-Treporti (VE)
comune.cavallinotreporti.ve.it

Apart from a few parked cars and tourists cycling to Lio Piccolo, th charming hamlet of Saccagnana feels like a journey back in time.

Near some of the houses, you'll find decidedly original installations such as fake windows framed with scallop shells and adorned wit curtains made from hundreds of cork stoppers. You'll also notice severa porcelain dolls in clean, well-kept clothes, sitting outside more than on dwelling.

The small Piazza del Prà is dominated by a particularly noteworth building: a three-storey palazzo dating from the first half of the 16t

entury. With its facade dominated by a stone staircase, the Zanella manor house has undergone various modifications over the years. Still, it retains its original form and serves as the focal point for the cluster of farmhouse-style buildings that give this place a magical atmosphere where time seems to stand still.

Saccagnana, whose name according to some derives from *grande secca* (large sandbank), was once known as Isola della Chiesa (Church Island), referring to the small oratory that falls under the parish jurisdiction of Santa Maria Assunta in Torcello, and is dedicated to the Holy Trinity. Built before the oratory in Treporti, it was the first church in the area.

NEARBY

Casa Rui: the convent with round chimneys ⑥

Via Via delle Mesole, 14
Cavallino-Treporti (VE)
comune.cavallinotreporti.ve.it
Can only be visited from the outside

Mesole is best reached by bicycle along a narrow road that cuts through the lagoon. The silence here is immediately striking, and it's the perfect setting for discovering a little treasure.

Mesole is a hamlet that's been inhabited since ancient times. It seems to have taken its name from a women's monastery established in 1380–81, probably identifiable with a structure known as Casa Rui or the Convent with Round Chimneys. What makes this building distinctive are its large, Alpine-style chimneys.

Despite its name, this wasn't necessarily a functioning convent. The term probably reflects ecclesiastical ownership rather than monastic occupation.

Various monasteries in Torcello and Murano owned areas of the lagoon that they used for agriculture or fish farming. In recent years, this area has become a favourite spot for hundreds of pink flamingos, which have made it one of their preferred locations during their time in the lagoon, from spring through to late summer.

CHIESA DEL CARMINE ALLE MESOLE

(7

Like being in a nice, cosy living room

Via delle Mesole, 14 – 30013 Cavallino-Treporti (VE)
Usually open during daytime hours

Arriving at Mesole, just before Casa Rui, there is a small buildin with a low bell tower. It is a 17th-century oratory, dedicated t Santa Maria del Carmine, like the one at Saccagnana.

The interior is intimate, with some benches and nice upholstere chairs, giving a feeling of a cosy living room. There is an altar with fres flowers, a small basin with Renaissance features and, on the walls, som ex-votos for graces received.

The Far Rivivere Mesole Association looks after and manages th little church and has signed a plaque at the entrance commemoratin the work done by Moreno Rigutto to restore the place to its forme glory.

On the right wall, as yo enter, is a Christ painted b Ramazzina Taurmina Alic Filomena Maurizia, a loca artist to whom the City o Jesolo has dedicated a stree in the Piazza Milano area opposite the Church of Sain Liberalis and Saint Maurus.

The oratory features in a list of churches of the northern lagoon compiled in 1620 by the Episcopal Chancellor of Torcello, and was originally dedicated to the Visitation of the Blessed Virgin. In 1685 the owner of the land and church was the Venetian patrician Gerolamo Correr di Riva San Biagio, but worshippers living nearby took care of the place. From the 19th century, the building appeared under the name Santa Maria del Carmine, a dedication probably inspired by the 16th-century painting of the *Madonna del Carmine with Child and Saints*, which replaced that of the *Virgin with Saints John the Baptist and Rocco*. In 1842, the oratory belonged to the Tacchella family.

Jujubes of Lio Piccolo

On the third Sunday of September, Lio Piccolo comes alive with a grand celebration. The 'Festa della Giuggiola' (Jujube Festival), organised by the Association of Lio Piccolo in collaboration with the Municipality of Cavallino-Treporti, has grown increasingly popular over the years. Alongside the area's cycle tourism routes, it has brought this small hamlet into the spotlight. The jujube tree has a long history in the Veneto region. Originally from Syria, it was introduced to Italy by the Romans under the name *Zyzyphus zizyphus*, a term that likely inspired the Venetian dialect word *zizoea*. However, it arrived in Venice later, with the intensification of trade with the East. It quickly found ideal growing conditions, particularly on the islands of Venice, the Euganean Hills, and the area around Lake Garda, where it can still be found today. The famous *brodo di giuggiole* is a very sweet liqueur typical of the Arquà Petrarca area (in the province of Padua). However, the phrase *andare in brodo di giuggiole* ('to go into jujube broth') is a figurative expression in Italian that denotes a state of great joy and delight. Today, the main area for jujube production is the northern Venetian coastline, including the Cavallino peninsula extending to Punta Sabbioni, Treporti, Lio Piccolo and Mesole. It is rare or found only as an ornamental plant in other coastal areas of the Venetian Lagoon and the central islands known for horticulture, even though the climatic conditions are very favourable for its cultivation.

CURIOSITIES OF LIO PICCOLO

Twenty or so inhabitants and an enchanting place

Via di Lio Piccolo
Cavallino-Treporti (VE)
Permanent exhibition "Frammenti di Laguna"
Saturday and Sunday 10am–noon and 3pm–5.30pm
Free admission

io Piccolo has been frequented since ancient times and was an important trading post as far back as the Roman era, as evidenced y the numerous archaeological finds here, including the remains of two rge warehouse houses with richly decorated mosaic floors.

There's much that could be written about Lio Piccolo: from the resence of the Boldù, a noble Venetian family, to the excellence of the jube fruits harvested here and celebrated each year during a week-long stival in September (see previous double page).

The distinctive character of Lio Piccolo led the Bolognese director ıd writer Pupi Avati to choose it as the setting for some of his Gothic ovels – *Il Signor Diavolo* and *L'archivio del diavolo* – both set in the small ımlet during the 1950s, when it was still inhabited by a considerable umber of people.

Every year, countless tourists reach this place by bicycle, stopping to dmire its landscapes or to sample delicious dishes prepared with the ırious crops grown here.

A very narrow strip of land leads to the heart of Lio Piccolo, where veral buildings face onto an open space: the little church, Palazzo oldù and the former nursery school building. Recently restored, the ursery now houses the permanent exhibition 'Frammenti di Laguna'. he exhibition displays archaeological finds recovered from the seabed f the northern lagoon and the surrounding area, spanning the Roman ge through the Middle Ages to the modern era.

The little church is worth a look. It dates from 1777, when the Boldù ımily became owners of the land and rebuilt the oratory on the site of ı earlier structure, consecrating it to Our Lady of the Snows.

In 1882, with the arrival of the Armenian Mekhitarist Fathers, the ıurch underwent significant modifications and a 22-metre bell tower 'as built, housing bells dedicated to the Virgin Mary, St Elizabeth and t Teresa.

The church interior lacks works of particular artistic significance, but has a welcoming atmosphere and contains one notable photograph: ardinal Angelo Giuseppe Roncalli (the future Pope John XXIII) uring a visit when he was Patriarch of Venice.

TOMBSTONE OF THE DAZIO, THE TOWN'S CUSTOMS

17th-century fares for transiting through locks

Via Cristo Re, 43 – 30016 Jesolo (VE)

In 1630 the Venetian Senate decreed to transfer the entry of boats coming from the Piave River into the northern lagoon, moving it from Lio Maggiore to Cavallino.

The decision was taken to preserve the lagoon basin from the transformations caused by the tides and the inflow of fresh water from the rivers flowing into it, which introduced a lot of debris, especially from occasional extraordinary floods.

Even the Sile River could be considered a danger: if the Piave broke its banks, it would pour its waters into it.

This occurred in 1533, and the Serenissima rushed to the rescue by implementing a series of changes to regulate the flows and prevent a repeat.

It made use of a special body, the Savi alle Acque (established in 1501 and flanked from 1531 by three enforcers), which implemented river regulations and hydraulic control throughout the territory.

The long events that led to the excavation of the Cavallino Canal (now called Casson Canal), and its locks in the Cavallino area, are part of this great work for the planning and protection of the northern lagoon.

The projects were implemented between the end of the 14th century and the 15th century and also concerned the navigation and transport of materials that passed through on their way to the lagoon.

We find concrete evidence of this not only in the locks still used today but also in the former customs building, which dates to 1632. Initially built in wood, it was replaced by a new one in masonry in 1654.

An example of the control and attention the Serenissima exerted on smuggling is the stone plaque placed on the building in 1668, which still shows the tariffs that were applied to transit through the locks.

Since its opening, the customs building also functioned as a tavern and was a meeting point for those who travelled along or near the waters. A charming inn still operates.

According to archives, there was also a small oratory dedicated to the Virgin Mary near the building, but there is no trace of it.

THE CRUCIFIX IN THE CHURCH CRISTO DEI SALSI

10

A miraculous crucifix

Via Cristo Re, 27 – Jesolo (VE)
Private property
Can be visited on 1 May every year, during the procession of Cristo dei Salsi

It is peculiar how a small church can lend its name to an entire road, yet that is the case here: 'Cristo Re' (Christ the King) is the name chosen to honour the crucifix housed within the religious building. The road bearing this name connects Jesolo to Cavallino.

Few are familiar with the story, which for centuries has been passed down orally rather than in written form.

The tale recounts that in the latter half of the 17th century, a farmer ploughing a field near the Jesolo marshes with his oxen was astonished to uncover a crucifix, half-buried in the soil. He loaded it onto his donkey and took it to the parish church of San Giovanni Battista, handing it to the parish priest, who stored it in a cupboard in the sacristy.

The next day, the farmer returned to the field to resume work. However, his oxen again inexplicably stopped, refusing to pull the plough.

To his amazement, he discovered another crucifix in the same field, identical to the one found the previous day. Again, he took the object to the parish priest, who attempted to place it alongside the first one in the cupboard. Yet, upon opening it, the first crucifix was gone. Word of the miraculous event quickly spread throughout the village.

The Zen family, owners of the land where the crucifix was found, decided to build a chapel in honour of Christ at the exact spot where they stumbled upon the crucifix. The small oratory there today is not the original – it is the result of a reconstruction carried out in 1964 on the original foundations.

The epithet 'dei Salsi' derives from the name of the locality where it is situated, now privately owned by the Montagner family.

Prominent personalities have visited the church, like Cardinal Albino Luciani, Patriarch of Venice from 1969 to 1978 (later Pope John Paul I), and Cardinal Marco Cé, Patriarch of Venice from 1978 to 2002.

THE PROCESSION OF CRISTO DEI SALSI

11

A moment of collective celebration

Every 1 May, at the Chiesa dei Salsi
After the 4pm Mass

The procession of the Cristo dei Salsi is a deeply cherished devotional event and its anniversary is celebrated every year with great enthusiasm.

Despite the crucifix's centuries-old history (see previous double page), it is taken out of the church once a year on 1 May for a brief but significant procession after the traditional Mass at 4pm.

Numerous seating arrangements are set up in the garden of the Montagner family to accommodate the large number of attendees, as the small church cannot hold everyone.

Typically, nearly all the residents of the hamlet and those originally from the area participate. The Mayor of Jesolo often attends, along with visitors from other towns.

At the end of the service, the crucifix is carefully removed from its wall mount and lowered to the ground, where it is entrusted to a designated custodian. It is then carried outside the church to begin the procession.

As per tradition, the procession takes place over a very short distance: about 150 metres and back again.

After passing through the garden path leading to the entrance gate, the crucifix is taken onto the road running along the embankment. For a few minutes, traffic is stopped as the officiating priest leads a moment of prayer, after which the priest blesses the hamlet and the River Sile, which flows less than 5 metres away.

The procession then returns to the church, where the crucifix is restored to its usual place on the wall, where it will remain for another year.

After, attendees gather for a moment of conviviality. It is tradition for everyone to bring something to eat, allowing participants to linger a while longer on the Montagner property and enjoy a moment of collective celebration outside the church.

TOWER OF CALIGO

12

Monitoring rivers and canals

Via Drago Jesolo - 30016 Jesolo (VE)
Can only be visited from outside

Of the five towers that stood in the medieval settlement of Equilum, only one has survived: the Turris Plave, better known the Tower of Caligo. They appear in historical maps and countless chive sources and were used to guard rivers and canals. Also, duties d taxes were levied there on passing vessels.

Because it was a strategic point connecting the River Sile with Venice d the Venetian Lagoon, the Caligo Canal was used for transiting bstantial commercial traffic, especially logs and timber from the region Cadore, and metal used for building and shipbuilding in Venice.

Towards the end of the 17th century, with the opening of the Porte Cavallino, traffic was moved further south and the tower fell into suse. Some sources claim it was intact in 1713, but it was probably owly dismantled in the following years to reuse its materials.

A number of sacred buildings also surrounded the building. There evidence from the mid-1500s of an oratory dedicated to Saint Peter, d the tower itself was probably used as a place of worship. A sort of bernacle, what remains of an altar and several crosses can be seen there.

On the outside, however, to the right of the entrance, some recent liefs of simple workmanship refer to Saint Romuald who, according to ne tradition, was housed in a monastery near the tower.

During World War I, the building was used as an ammunition depot y soldiers fighting along the Piave front.

In 1927, an iron cross from the old church of San Donà, destroyed uring the Great War, was placed on the highest wall.

Today it is a protected archaeological site that can be reached by car, cycle or on foot.

PONTOON BRIDGE AT CAPOSILE

One of eight pontoon bridges still in operation in Italy

Toll charges for vehicles (during certain hours)
ATVO bus: lines 10A–118

)ontoon bridges are undeniably fascinating, and only eight remain in Italy. Three of them are in Veneto, within a few kilometres of each her.

One is at Caposile, a hamlet in the municipality of San Donà di Piave, ry close to the north-western edge of the lagoon.

Interestingly, Caposile got its name after 1683, when the Serenissima verted the River Sile. Instead of letting it flow into Portegrandi, they annelled it into the old bed of the River Piave. This is why the River le flows for many kilometres parallel to the lagoon, separated by just a urrow strip of land.

The Caposile Bridge connects Via IV Novembre and Via dei Salsi. uilt in the 1960s, it consists of a steel deck resting on five concrete ontoons.

The structure is designed so that, when needed – during certain hours id by appointment – it can be rotated to allow boats to pass along the nal.

However, the bridge's primary function is to provide direct access to lsi, saving local residents from a lengthy detour through Jesolo.

Other pontoon bridges in Italy

There are seven other pontoon bridges in Italy: two in the province of Mantua (at Torre d'Oglio and Commessaggio), one in the province of Pavia (at Bereguardo), and two within the Po Delta Regional Park (at Po di Goro and Po di Gnocca).

In Veneto, besides Caposile, there are two other pontoon bridges: one at Cortellazzo and another in the municipality of Noventa di Piave, just a few kilometres away. In operation since 1951, the Ponte Zamuner is the modern successor to an ancient ferry that has been documented since the 13th century.

DRAWBRIDGE AT CAPOSILE

An original bridge

Via Castaldia, Caposile (VE)
ATVO bus: lines 10A–118

Built between 1925 and 1927 based on a design by engineer Giuseppe Pasquali, the remarkable drawbridge at Caposile spans e final stretch of the Piave Vecchia.

Despite being nearly a century old, the structure remains completely tact and is constantly maintained: the mechanism still works (though) barges requiring its opening still pass through here), and since 1957 – hen the current road crossing over the Piave Vecchia was inaugurated – e bridge has been open only to pedestrians and cyclists.

The bridge operated thanks to a drawbridge mechanism, still present day, which used a series of counterweights to open and allow boats d barges to pass through.

Because of its shape, it has often been compared to the Langlois idge near Arles in France, which became famous as a recurring subject several works by Vincent van Gogh dating from 1888.

The Caposile bridge has been dedicated to General Armando Diaz, hief of Staff of the Royal Army during the Great War, who organised e defence of the Italian front along the banks of the Piave.

Close by stands the Monument to the Fallen Financiers, built tween 1989 and 1993. The monument serves as a reminder that this ea witnessed bloody clashes during the First World War.

A panel on the bridge's southern bank lists the names of the ttalions which, in November 1917, fought right here '... to save nice, sustaining a furious battle against the enemy and leaving on the ound an as yet unknown number of fallen'.

THE ARCHAEOLOGICAL AREA OF ALTINO

Open-air remains of the ancient city

Strada Provinciale Quarto D'Altino Porte, 43 – 30020 Altino VE
+39 0422 789443
drm-ven.museoaltino@cultura.gov.it
Tuesday to Saturday 8am to 7pm, Sunday and bank holidays 2pm to 7pm, closed Monday
ATVO bus: line 25A

Just 500 metres from the National Archaeological Museum of Altino (see p. 52), you'll find two beautiful archaeological areas perfect for interesting walk.

The first area shows the Augustan residential quarter – part of the cient city built alongside a stretch of *decumanus* (main road), where u can still see traces of villas and public buildings, including the unning mosaic of the *Domus della Pantera* (House of the Panther).

The other area reveals the remains of a landing dock and a onumental gate dating from the first half of the 1st century BCE.

Visitors could enter Altinum directly from the water through two tes like this one, arriving straight onto the cardo, one of the city's ain streets.

Today you can see the foundations of this entrance structure, which st on oak timber piling. You can clearly make out the base of one of e two octagonal towers that flanked the entrance.

The 60 or so people who still live in Altino today have plenty of ories about archaeological discoveries in the area. Pietro Calza has one the best stories to tell: He was working his land when he found a eautiful pure gold necklace from Roman times – you can now see it at e Archaeological Museum.

BOAT IN THE CHURCH OF ST HELIODORUS

A unique church designed by its own parishioners

Via S. Eliodoro, 29
30020 Quarto d'Altino VE
ATVO bus: line 25A

Built in 1961, the Church of St Heliodorus in Altino wasn't design by an architect. Instead, local residents came up with the idea a wanted it built themselves – many even brought their own belongin and created the artwork inside.

Above the entrance door, you'll be surprised to see a real boat – *saltafossi* – with its middle section wrapped in netting. This type of bo was typical in the marshy areas between the Sile and Piave rivers. I very versatile, similar to a *sandolo* but much simpler in design, perfe for use in ditches, rivers, marshes and lagoon waters.

The boat shows how attached the people of Altino are to the Veni Lagoon. For many of them, fishing there was their source of liveliho and income.

With many locals also working as sharecroppers, the church h many references to the land.

Near the altar, a large cross was made entirely from soy cane The pulpit is made from a tree trunk placed upside down. Its roo point upward – just as trees in nature get nourishment from the eart

hurchgoers get spiritual nourishment from the Holy Scriptures, specially the gospel.

The base of the raised platform where the altar stands is surrounded y rope, reminding us that, just as hemp fibres form a strong cord, ndividual people joining together can create a resilient and strong ommunity.

Above the two confessionals by the entrance are brambles made from nulberry branches from the nearby countryside. These represent the nots that worshippers feel they need to untie through reconciliation.

The holy water font is made from a Roman archaeological find – a tone bowl set into tree bark.

Since the early 1980s, the church has housed two bone fragments of Saint Heliodorus (around 407 CE), to whom the church is dedicated. After becoming the first Bishop of Altino, Saint Heliodorus spent his final years in Torcello, where he died. He was initially buried in Altino, but when the people there left the city and began dismantling buildings to reuse materials, Saint Heliodorus' remains were moved again to Torcello, to the Basilica of Santa Maria Assunta, where they rest today.

For husbands fighting at the front

Near the altar stands a wooden statue of the Madonna, bought in 1942 by a group of women from Altino hoping to place their husbands, sons and relatives fighting at the front under Mary's protection.

NATIONAL ARCHAEOLOGICAL MUSEUM OF ALTINO 17

Discovering the Roman city on the Venice Lagoon

Via S. Eliodoro, 56 – 30020 Quarto d'Altino VE
0422 789443
drm-ven.museoaltino@cultura.gov.it
Tuesday to Saturday from 8am to 7pm, Sunday and bank holidays from 2pm t
7pm, closed Monday
ATVO bus: line 25A

We highly recommend a visit to Altino for history and archaeology enthusiasts.

The ideal place to begin an interesting journey of discovery is the National Archaeological Museum, a site most tourists don't know about. This is where you'll find the most important discoveries from this fascinating ancient city that once stood on the lagoon.

The first rooms to visit are housed in a 19th-century rural building, restored and incorporated into a larger complex featuring new structures completed in 2014.

The ground floor has two sections telling the story of prehistoric life along the lagoon edges, where Altino would eventually be built. You'll see Iron Age artefacts and learn about religion, language, early settlements, writing systems and burial practices of the time.

On the first floor, you can see the city's transformations under Roman rule, from the 2nd century BCE to the 3rd century CE, with detailed explanations of urbanisation, roads, fashion, notable figures of the time, trade and society.

There's a feature that will catch the eye of more observant visitors, which restoration has preserved in its original state: along the walls you can see numerous inscriptions, mainly noted in pencil, dating to the 1800s when the building served as a farm and rice mill.

Inside another building leading to a small tower, you can visit the *MostrAttiva Antenati altinati* (Active Exhibition of Altino Ancestors), which displays some funerary sculptures, formerly part of the Guarienti collection and recently acquired. Don't miss a relief that went missing around 1950, rediscovered in 2017 by the Carabinieri Cultural Heritage Protection Unit of Venice, unfortunately with some missing parts.

Altino was one of the first cities in north-eastern Italy to have a bishop, and it faced disaster twice: first when Attila's Huns destroyed it in 452 CE, then again when the Lombards conquered and likely destroyed it from 635–639 CE. These attacks forced the survivors to flee to the lagoon islands, especially Torcello. This migration marked the start of the long historical process that would eventually lead to the birth of Venice.

TOWER OF TESSERA

(18)

A medieval tower that became the bell tower of nearby Sant'Elena Church

Via Triestina – 30173 Tessera VE
torre-antica.tessera@libero.it
Can only be visited from the outside
Church: visits every Thursday 4pm–6pm

ocated close to Venice's Marco Polo International Airport, the medieval tower of Tessera is often overlooked.

Standing 24 metres tall with a 14-metre circumference at its base, is Roman–Byzantine-influenced tower was built between the 9th d 10th centuries. It was probably constructed for defensive, military d lookout purposes, making it one of Mestre's oldest monuments. Its nstruction from altinelle (small stones) suggests the building materials ely came from the nearby Altino area.

Later, it became the bell tower for the neighbouring Church of nt'Elena, which was connected to a Benedictine monastery. Thanks Gregorio Giustiniani, the bishop of Treviso, it became an abbey in 139 and was dedicated to Sant'Elena, under the rule of Matilde di anossa.

Today, the bell chamber houses two small bronze bells – you can read e casting date of 1509 on one of them.

On the church facade, an inscription dated 1507 remembers Abbot revisan, who revived the church and the monastery with the help of e friars of San Cipriano in Murano.

The church and tower belong to the Checchin family (known as adi'), who bought them at auction in July 1869.

The complex is currently for sale, but local associations and residents ope for a new use that will preserve its historical and artistic value.

EARBY

he tower of Dese

ia Cimitero di Dese – 30173 Dese VE

an only be visited from the outside

n the Favaro municipality area at Dese, you'll find another medieval ower of about 20 metres tall.

THE SPOTTER'S BENCH

A meeting point for aviation enthusiasts

Via Bazzera – 30173 Tessera VE
Accessible by car or on foot from the town centre

Near every major airport, there's a favourite spot for people who love watching planes land and take off – whether to photograph them, ppreciate their technical details or simply daydream.

In Tessera, the Venice district where the Marco Polo International irport is located, just a few metres from Fort Bazzera, you'll find a learing with a bench nicknamed 'the spotter's bench'. It faces the goon – or rather, the airport runways.

The view from this observation point is spectacular. You can easily see lanes landing and planes beginning their take-off run. The backdrop Venice's skyline with its many bell towers, domes and the silhouettes f major churches.

Almost every aircraft model that made aviation history has passed hrough this stretch of lagoon: from the Lockheed L-049 Constellation the Boeing 707 (including Air Force One configuration), from the IcDonnell Douglas DC-10 to the Antonov An-124, from the Boeing 47 to Concorde.

Currently, daily traffic averages between 230 and 240 aircraft novements.

The planes you'll see most often are Airbus A319s and A320s, plus arious versions of the Boeing 737.

The largest aircraft model currently operating daily flights is the oeing 777-300ER.

GIANCARLO FERRACINA HISTORICAL DOCUMENTATION LABORATORY

20

A small but wonderful museum

Piazzale Bernardino Zendrini, 36 – 30173 Campalto VE
terraantica.org
September to end of May, weekdays only
ACTV bus: lines 5 – 9 – 13

On the first floor of Don Milani Primary School in Campalto's Villaggio Laguna district, there's a remarkable little place born om genuine passion for local heritage and a determination to save ecious memories before they slip away forever.

Created and maintained by the 'Terra Antica' Association, the storical documentation laboratory is dedicated to Giancarlo Ferracina, 10 was the school's head teacher for almost 20 years.

The visitor route recreates typical Veneto household rooms from e 1900s, with a kitchen, bedroom, cellar and a corner dedicated to ildren and studying.

The rooms are furnished with original objects that create the illusion stepping back in time: tools used by cobblers, pots and pans, spinning uipment, everyday objects of all kinds, and photographs. Everything kes you back to country houses where every corner was put to good e. One section focuses on farm work and livestock, with typical tools ed for fieldwork.

A special section is devoted to the Campalto lagoon shore area and goon fishing.

The Terra Antica Association, which maintains and promotes this ace, was founded in 1992. It deals with everything related to the cal area, organising exhibitions of physical documents and archive aterials, photography shows and cultural, educational and recreational tivities, often involving other cultural and sports associations. It has ıblished various books.

Public visits are only possible on weekdays during the school term, om September to the end of May. This small but wonderful museum tracts many visitors of all ages: from primary school pupils to university udents, to independent groups wanting to discover their grandparents' ıst by examining original pieces collected by the association and other olunteers.

STATUE AT THE OSSUARY OF FORTE MARGHERA

A place commemorating the victims of the 1849 sieg

Via Forte Marghera, 30 – Mestre (VE)
ACTV bus: lines 9-9H-12-15-43-80

Adjacent to the Historical Museum (see opposite) stands a sm ossuary that commemorates the massacre carried out by t Austrians during their fierce assault on Forte Marghera in May 1849.

In a final, desperate act of resistance, the Venetians emerged fro the fort at first light on 27 October 1848 to attack Mestre, managing liberate it from the Austrians.

After very quickly reoccupying the town, the Austrians besieg the fort with an army of almost 30,000 men under the command General Haynau, bombarding it with artillery until May the followi year, when the troops withdrew towards Venice.

Once inside the fort, the Austrians buried the dead in a mass grav A plaque has been placed here in memory of their sacrifice.

Inside the shrine to those who fell in the uprisings of 1848/4 you can see the work entitled *Fante di schegge* (Infantry of Shrapne inaugurated in 2018 a created by sculptor Carlucc Zangirolami using shrapn fragments recovered fro various First World W battlefields.

The statue depicts Italian infantryman wh having set down his rucksa at the end of the conflict, loo to the future – towards a ne world waiting to be rebuilt.

The work was acquired the museum on the centena of the end of the First Wor War.

ɅILITARY HISTORY MUSEUM ⑳22
)F FORTE MARGHERA

little-known site dedicated to history and military istory enthusiasts

a Forte Marghera, 30 – Mestre (VE) –Forte Marghera – blokhaus Lunetta VI
9 3396821709 – museofortemarghera.it
ɔening hours: according to calendar
ee admission
CTV bus: lines 9–9H–12–15–43–80

orte Marghera is a former military complex covering more than 48 hectares (including canals) that was part of the Entrenched Camp of ıestre. Here you'll find the International Centre for the Promotion of ɔrtified Historical Heritage, as well as a Military History Museum and a nall ossuary – both virtually unknown to most visitors.

The museum was established by passionate employees of the Army's h Supply Unit and is now run by an association that safeguards its tegrity and public access. It houses weapons, working tools, medical uipment for field hospitals, various memorabilia and a photographic chive. Outside, there are several cannons and various military vehicles, cluding a depot train, ammunition, a military engineers' steamroller ıd a curious mobile bakery mounted on two van trailers. This last piece particularly interesting: inside it contains everything needed to make ead, from the oven (powered by a diesel burner) to the mixing machine, om the divider to the proofing chamber.

Every year the museum's activities conclude in early December with ceremony held on the Feast of St Barbara, patron saint of those who ork with fire and related fields, such as artillerymen, explosives experts, ıgineers, sailors and firefighters.

The tradition of honouring St Barbara at Forte Marghera dates ıck to 1951, when the eadquarters of the Venice rtillery Directorate, established in 1866 on the 'and of San Giorgio, was ansferred to the Fort.)n that occasion, a commemorative wreath was id at the small cemetery here the remains of those ho fell during the 1849 ege are preserved.

A WALK AROUND FORTE MARGHERA

Military heritage and nature away from the crowds

Forte Marghera
Mestre (VE)
Free admission
ACTV bus: lines 9-9H-12-15-43-80

Built between 1805 and 1842, Forte Marghera served exclusive for military purposes for around 150 years and formed part of t lagoon's wider defence system.

It now belongs to the City of Venice, which has opened it to t public. Various restoration and regeneration projects are under wa some already completed, others in progress.

A stroll around this place, barely visible and known mainly residents of Mestre and the surrounding area, is highly recommend for anyone interested in studying decommissioned and repurpos military sites, for those wanting to immerse themselves in the nature a place experiencing new life, and for families looking for a safe spa

·here children can run and play freely – there's no vehicle traffic inside ıis vast complex.

Besides the Military History Museum (see p. 61), the outer perimeter f Forte Marghera incorporates the only surviving structure from the riginal village of Marghera: three arches of a 16th-century bridge now eneath a building, where marker stone no. 71 records that the fort lies ·ithin the lagoon basin.

In the internal canal you can see what remains of an old transport oat.

There's also a cat colony managed by the Mici del Forte Association, vhich voluntarily cares for over 200 cats, rescuing them from life as trays and potential acts of violence.

Forte Marghera is an artistic venue too: it hosts concerts and, in ıe Palmanova Pavilion, artistic residencies, workshops and research rojects take place.

It also houses a pavilion of the Venice Biennale's International Art Exhibition.

In the past, it has hosted an exhibition of 20th-century Italian nd international sculptural works from the International Gallery of Modern Art at Ca' Pesaro in Venice.

THE ISLAND OF SAN SECONDO

2

A stop on an island that housed a Benedictine monastery, a military fort and an explosives factory

Accessible only by private boat

From the Ponte della Libertà, the island of San Secondo is seen dail by thousands of commuters: a forgotten patch of land, a sma island covered in dense vegetation that conceals its true form. Venetia jokingly call it the Island of Coats because the sight of it signals arriv at Santa Lucia railway station.

Others mistakenly refer to it as the Island of Cannons, due to its oximity to a monument (featuring two period cannons) beside the ilway bridge, dedicated to those who fell during the Austrian siege in ne 1849.

Accessible by boat, the island of San Secondo is occasionally used as pit stop by those exploring the lagoon by boat or kayak.

Originally dedicated to Sant'Erasmo, the island changed its name in 237 with the arrival of the relics of San Secondo of Asti.

The Benedictine community already present in 1529 was transferred Giudecca by order of Pope Clement VII and the monastery was ppressed, probably due to the nuns' libertine conduct.

In 1535, the Dominican order took over, restoring the existing uildings and remaining until 1806.

During the plague years (1630/1631), it housed members of the rench ambassador's family, and not a single case of illness was recorded n the island.

In 1686, it became a college for clerics of the Dominican observance.

In 1824 the church was demolished, the body of San Secondo ansferred (it's currently in Venice, at the church of the Gesuati), and e other buildings were converted for military use.

The island was transformed into an octagonal fort that became part f the military outpost of the San Marco Defence Line, designed to rotect San Giuliano, the city of Venice and, after its construction, the ilway bridge from potential attacks.

In 1848 the island was heavily bombarded by the Austro–Hungarians.

In the early 1900s, it was used as a checkpoint for the new power line aching the San Giobbe district in Venice from Campalto.

During the war years, it was used by Junghans, officially as a fireworks ctory. In reality, bombs and mines built at the Giudecca factory were aded with explosives here.

After the Second World War, it was leased to a caretaker and took n the popular name Island of Cows, as farmyard animals were raised here. It was subsequently abandoned and has remained in its current ate ever since.

Today you can still see the remains of a roofless military structure on e island, where restoration projects are occasionally carried out.

THE ISLAND OF CAMPALTO

The last of the eight military batteries still 'usable'

Accessible only by private boat

Also known as Batteria Campalto, the island is named after th nearby village of Campalto on the lagoon shore.

This island was part of the defensive system conceived by th Venetians in the final years of the Republic of Venice, the so-calle Serenissima, and was subsequently strengthened during foreign ru (French and Austrian). It was also used by the Italian armed forc during both world wars, primarily as an anti-aircraft position or rad base.

During its military history, the island's layout was quite similar that of the other batteries (Buel del Lovo, Tessera, Carbonera, Trezz Campana, Ex Poveglia, Fisolo): partly polygonal and partly semicircula with one building serving as a small barracks, another as a powd

ıagazine, and a small breakwater around its perimeter to protect it om potential raids.

In the 1920s, the island became home to five families from 'annaregio who had been evacuated to Emilia-Romagna during ıe First World War. In 1929, during a severe freeze, a fire brigade :ebreaker had to reach Campalto to rescue a family from the cold and ood shortages.

After being permanently decommissioned by the armed forces in the 960s (the anti-aircraft battery had already been dismantled in 1946), ıe island was converted into a landfill site.

The waste it received came primarily from Murano's glass furnaces nd workshops.

Restoration work on the island was completed in 1998. A jetty was dded in 2005, making the island easily accessible for those who explore he lagoon in traditional boats, canoes or kayaks.

Because it remains publicly accessible and has tables, benches and helters for visitors who wish to spend a few hours here, Campalto is the ıst of the eight batteries that can still be genuinely experienced.

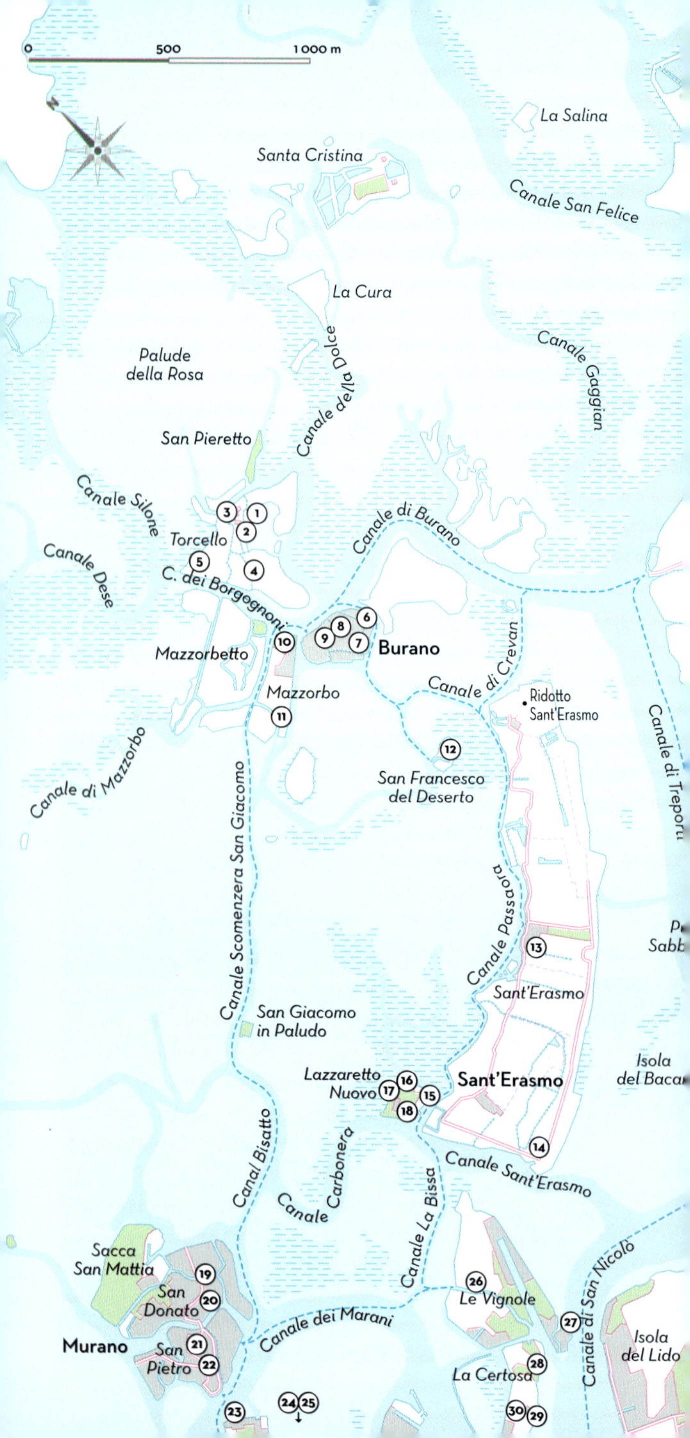
0
500
1 000 m
La Salina
Santa Cristina
Canale San Felice
La Cura
Canale della Dolce
Canale Gaggian
Palude
della Rosa
San Pieretto
Canale Silone
Torcello
Canale Dese
C. dei Borgognoni
Canale di Burano
Burano
Mazzorbetto
Mazzorbo
Canale di Crevan
Ridotto
Sant'Erasmo
Canale di Treporti
San Francesco
del Deserto
Canale di Mazzorbo
Canale Scomenzera San Giacomo
Canale Passaora
Sant'Erasmo
San Giacomo
in Paludo
Lazzaretto
Nuovo
Sant'Erasmo
Isola
del Bacan
Canal Bisatto
Canale Carbonera
Canale La Bissa
Canale Sant'Erasmo
Sacca
San Mattia
San
Donato
Murano
San
Pietro
Canale dei Marani
Le Vignole
Canale di San Nicolò
Isola
del Lido
La Certosa
1
2
3
4
5
6
7
8
9
10
11
12
13
14
15
16
17
18
19
20
21
22
23
24
25
26
27
28
29
30

North-Central Lagoon

ORATORY OF ST MARK IN TORCELLO

The place where St Mark's relics may have rested for a night

Island of Torcello, behind the Basilica of Santa Maria Assunta
Accessible by public transport: lines 9, 12

n Torcello, behind the better-known Basilica of Santa Maria Assunta, stands a small rectangular building with exposed brick walls and a tile of. Most visitors walk straight past it, but this humble oratory is said mark the spot where, according to tradition, the relics of St Mark e Evangelist were received for one night after being brought to the goon from the East by Buono da Malamocco and Rustico da Torcello. ccording to some legends, it was Rustico himself who had this little urch built at his own expense. Historically, on 25 April – the saint's feast ay – a simple procession would make its way to the oratory.

NEARBY

tone balconies of the Basilica of Torcello: false egends ②

orcello, Basilica di Santa Maria Assunta – Vaporetto: linee 9, 12

lany myths circulate around the lagoon area, and some concern those eculiar balconies on the south nave of the Basilica of Torcello. One tale laims they were used to close off the building to defend against enemy ttacks; another suggests they were sealed during winter to keep out the old. In reality, these false balconies are part of the modifications the tructure underwent in the 9th century, when major restoration work ook place. They serve no function other than aesthetic.

CARLO PICCOLI'S GARDEN

A little paradise

Torcello, opposite the Basilica
Private residence, not open to visitors
Vaporetto: lines 9, 12

Right opposite the Basilica of Torcello is a garden that's impossible to miss. Many tourists and curious onlookers poke their noses and meras through the railings to capture a few shots of this place that ems to have come straight out of a fairytale.

Vine-covered arches, classical statues among colourful flowers – it's the result of the work and passion of Carlo Piccoli, a Venice antique ealer who made his Torcello house his workplace and a little paradise r art lovers, embellishing the garden with statues and bas-reliefs.

His daughter Nicoletta, a spirited woman with as much love for art her father, carries on his dream, living most of the year on this island at now has just 12 inhabitants.

There's not only art in this garden but plenty of history too: the vines e of a particular species native to the island, the renowned Dorona ape.

ISLAND OF SAN GIOVANNI EVANGELISTA

The remains of the women's monastery of San Giovanni Evangelista, founded before the year 1000

Island of Torcello
Visits by appointment
info@sangiovannitorcello.com

For many visitors, a trip to Torcello ends with the Basilica and Archaeological Museum, and they head straight back to the landing age, perhaps after a quick look at the Devil's Bridge.

However, if you cross the bridge and follow the path, you'll reach the land of San Giovanni. Here you can see the remains of the women's onastery of San Giovanni Evangelista, founded before the year 1000 ıd demolished after its closure in 1810.

In the 1960s, the Superintendency of Antiquities of the Veneto gion conducted an archaeological excavation that brought to light veral construction phases of the religious building, still visible today.

What remains of the original complex – besides some sections of the erimeter walls – is a Gothic building created from what was once the ıesthouse, restored in the mid-20th century after serving as a dwelling ır fishermen and farmers.

The monastery's origins are probably linked to the island's aristocratic milies, particularly that of Doge Pietro Orseolo II, whose children ere Felicita, Abbess of the Monastery of San Giovanni, and Orso rseolo, Bishop of Torcello.

In 1009, the remains of St Barbara of Nicomedia were received ere, donated a few years earlier by Maria Argyropolis – niece of the yzantine emperor and sister-in-law of the then abbess, Felicita – to her ıurch. The relics were moved during the Napoleonic era and placed in ıe church of San Martino in Burano, where they remain.

CASA MUSEO ANDRICH

The Lovers' House of the Lagoon

Isola di Torcello
Visits by appointment only: call well in advance on 0335 5228854
The visit may be cancelled at the last moment
Vaporetto: line 9, 12

On the island of Torcello, the 'artist's house' dedicated to Luc Andrich is one of the lagoon's best-kept secrets. Today, we a fortunate to admire it thanks to Paolo Andrich, his nephew, who work tirelessly to preserve this space imbued with the artistic spirit of the 195 60s and 70s before his untimely passing in 2021. While the museu interior will leave you in awe, the exterior is even more captivating: garden designed by the artist himself, highlighting vegetable plots and a orchard while also preserving the historic vineyard. This is a true have for those seeking the perfect balance between art and nature, seamless blending into a setting that is truly one of a kind.

Born in 1927, Lucio Andrich was orphaned at a young age an took over managing the family haberdashery, where he developed deep passion for textiles. While recovering from a war injury at th pulmonology hospital on the island of Sacca Sessola, he met his futu wife, Clementina De Luca. Together, they attended the Academy of Fin Arts in Venice, where he became the last professor of mosaic art before th discipline was removed from the curriculum.

After living for a time in Venice at Palazzo Carminati, Andric relocated to the island of Torcello, residing first in a house that had onc been the sacristy of the ancient Church of St Thomas of the Burgundian and later at the Vignagranda Fort in the Palude della Rosa. This fort no houses the museum dedicate to his legacy.

Andrich was undoubtedl a versatile artist: a painte engraver, graphic designe sculptor and creator c designs for a wide range c artistic techniques. He ofte collaborated with his belove wife, who brought many c his designs to life as tapestrie many of which adorn thei home – affectionately know by many as 'The Lovers House of the Lagoon'.

The chiari: *moons of the salt marsh*

Salt marshes of the northern lagoon
Accessible by private boat only

Perfect symmetrical circles in the middle of the salt marshes, only fully visible from the air, are not a sight you'd expect to find in the lagoon! These circular formations are a delightful surprise when you spot them, and immediately beg the question: natural phenomenon or man-made?

As strange as it may sound, they're entirely natural. Known as *chiari*, these circular pools form in depressions where brackish lagoon water and rainwater come together.

The *chiari* shown here lie on a salt marsh in the northern lagoon, close to Burano, though they appear in other parts of the lagoon as well.

If you're lucky enough to fly over the lagoon – whether by plane or helicopter, or departing from Marco Polo Airport – look down at the salt marshes and you'll almost certainly spot some of these curious formations!

THE HOUSE OF REMIGIO BARBARO

6

Burano's only uncoloured house

Burano, Località Terranova, Calle Gobbi 79–80
Can only be visited from the outside
Vaporetto: line 12

Remigio Barbaro's house-studio is the only uncoloured building on the island. Protected by the Ministry of Culture, it was once open to visitors after restoration and maintenance works, but unfortunately the interior is no longer accessible.

Many hope this unique place will reopen. For now, it stands out from Burano's brightly painted houses thanks to the works of art displayed outside.

The property is impossible to miss: along the garden perimeter runs St Francis's famous quotation *Laudato sie, mi' Signore, cum tutte le Tue creature* ('Praised be You, my Lord, with all Your creatures'). Through the greenery, you can glimpse several sculptures, including a striking St Francis opposite the entrance – naked, mouth wide open, gaze turned heavenward – and a study for the bronze statue of Baldassarre Galuppi that stands in Burano's piazza of the same name.

The artist lived a simple, unassuming life here with his wife Giovannina. Some have called him 'Franciscan' or even a 'hermit', reflecting his solitary existence devoted to spiritual exploration – a quality evident in his art, which largely centred on religious subjects.

Remigio Barbaro died in 2005, having spent his lifetime envisioning what was to become his personal museum. Visitors often described his house as a 'paradise' – a space brimming with art objects and dreams that embodied the mystical fusion of art, nature and spirituality he recreated in his work.

Many of his terracotta pieces, bronzes, drawings, studies and models remain inside the house, while others are held in private collections and sites across the surrounding area including: the Basilica of Torcello, the Church of Santa Fosca, the Convent of San Francesco del Deserto, St Mark's Basilica, the Cà Pesaro Museum, and in Cavallino, where his statue graces the War Memorial in Piazza Santa Maria Elisabetta. His work also appears in Burano's Church of San Martino, at the entrance to Mazzorbo cemetery, and in the cemeteries of San Michele in Venice, Mestre and the Venice Lido.

Two other sculptures can be found in Burano itself: *Attesa di pace* (Waiting for Peace) beside the vaporetto landing stage, and the statue of Baldassare Galuppi in the piazza.

MOSAIC OF ST BARBARA IN BURANO AND THE EMPIRE STATE BUILDING

7

St Barbara in New York

Scuola dei Pescatori, Burano
Daily: 8am–noon and 3pm–7pm
Vaporetto: line 12

Inside the chapel dedicated to St Barbara at the Scuola dei Pescator (Fishermen's School) – where her relics rest – you'll find a highl unusual mosaic created by the Ravenna Mosaic School. It depicts S

arbara supporting one of New York's most iconic skyscrapers: the mpire State Building.

A similar mosaic – this time showing the saint holding up the bell ower of Burano's Church of San Martino – can be found at the Church f Our Saviour on Park Avenue in New York.

Both works were commissioned as part of the celebrations marking ne bicentenary of St Barbara's relics arriving on the lagoon island in 011 (see below), creating a symbolic link between the two cities.

The relics had already travelled to New York in 2008 when they vere taken to Ground Zero – the site of the former Twin Towers – as a ymbolic message of universal peace.

This came about after a specific request from firefighters of Italian escent working in New York, for whom St Barbara is the patron saint.

St Barbara's remains arrived in the Big Apple with full honours, hose normally reserved for a head of state. A moving service followed n memory of the firefighters who lost their lives in the terrorist attack f 11 September 2001.

After a week, the relics returned to Burano.

St Barbara, the martyr who rests in Burano

According to legend, the relics of St Barbara were brought to Venice in 1009 and placed in the church of San Giovanni Evangelista in Torcello. Following its closure under Napoleon Bonaparte (1806), the saint's remains were transferred to the presbyterial church of San Martino in Burano on 10 March 1811. In 1926, the remains were moved from the parish church to the small oratory. The story goes that St Barbara was a beautiful young woman and, to hide her from the world, her father locked her in a tower. After converting to Christianity, she had a third window built into her tower to symbolise the Trinity. Her father, enraged, had her breasts cut off and then beheaded her: he was immediately struck by lightning and reduced to ashes. Not knowing her baptismal name, the Christians who recovered her body called her 'the barbarian young woman' (in ancient Greek, *barbaros* simply meant 'foreigner'), from which her name derives. Her feast day is celebrated on 4 December. She's the patron saint of professions linked to fire (firefighters, artillerymen, miners and explosives experts) because of her symbolic associations with fire, lightning and explosions. Though legend places her birth around 235 CE under the Roman emperor Maximinus I near Nicomedia (now Izmir in Turkey), her very existence is widely questioned today.

HIDDEN CHAPEL OF THE VIA DELLA VIGNA

8

A buranello jewel

Via della Vigna, Burano
Visible from the outside
Vaporetto: line 12

This is one of those places that, although it is in the public eye, almost always goes unnoticed.

To find it, simply leave the more well-known Lace Museum to the left and take Via della Vigna: you will find it on your right, in a small burgundy building whose entrance is surmounted by a 16th-century bas-relief depicting a holy bishop.

The chapel is closed by a heavy wrought-iron and glass door and through the small door, you will discover a beautiful, almost life-size Madonna, which was in the church of San Martino until the 1960s. At least, that is what the custodian of the small chapel remembers.

This statue of the Virgin in prayer, hands folded, without the child in her arms as classical iconography would have it, looks like a bride adorned in a dress of Burano lace made entirely by hand.

It is rare to find the door open to admire this little Burano jewel, but during May it is possible to attend the evening rosary and experience a little of that special Marian devotion that so characterises the people of the lagoon.

Plaque in honour of Gino Rossi

Near the vaporetto landing is a plaque which commemorates the important connection between Luigi Rossi, a 'forgotten artist', and the island of Burano.

Rossi's unique style was shaped by his exposure to the art of the Nabis, Van Gogh and Gauguin, discovered during his travels, often in the company of his more renowned friend, Arturo Martini. Born into a well-off Venetian family on 6 June 1884, Rossi became a leading figure in a Venetian artistic revival known as the 'School of Burano'.

Rossi, familiarly called 'Gino', attended school in Florence and the prestigious Foscarini Lyceum in Venice, but left formal education at 14 to devote himself entirely to his passion for painting. Biographical details are sparse, though it is known he married fellow artist Bice Levi Minzi in 1903 and studied privately with the Russian painter Schereschewskj, who occupied a studio in Palazzo Pesaro in 1905.

Two significant trips between 1906 and 1909, to Paris and Great Britain, and participations in the Venice Biennale in 1908 and 1909, were instrumental in shaping Rossi's artistic vision.

Rossi settled down permanently in Burano and made his mark with other Burano-based painters in 1913. That year, after being excluded from the Biennale, the Burano-based painters exhibited at Ca' Pesaro, signalling their disapproval of the political climate and promoting peaceful coexistence and harmony with both the past and nature, while embracing European avant-garde movements of the time. The exhibition's censorship by the municipality drew attention from prominent figures in the art world. Sadly, this politically charged stance against conflict likely contributed to the obscurity of the School of Burano.

In 1915, Rossi left Burano for Ciano sul Montello. During the war, he served on the front lines, was captured and held as a prisoner of war in Rastatt, Germany, an ordeal that profoundly affected his body and mind. Upon returning, he found his hillside home destroyed, and moved with his mother to Noventa Padovana. Financial struggles slowed his artistic output, and his work adopted a more Cézanne-inspired Cubist style as his physical and mental health deteriorated.

Ultimately, Rossi was institutionalised, first at the psychiatric hospital in Mogliano, then on San Clemente Island in Venice, and finally at Sant'Artemio in Treviso, where he passed away in 1947.

HOUSE OF BEPI SUÀ

During summer evenings, he organised a small open-air cinema in the campiello where he lived

Calle del Pistor, 399
Burano
info@casabepi.it
Vaporetto: line 12

ı Burano, colourful houses abound, but one in particular catches the ɜye of anyone passing by: the Casa di Bepi Suà.

This vibrant home belonged to Giuseppe Toselli (1920–2002), ıown locally as Bepi Suà.

Bepi worked as a maintenance man at the Cinema Favin, but when e cinema closed, he inherited the old hand-crank projector and invented himself.

His passion for cinema was evident. By day, he sold sweets in the azza, and on summer evenings, he transformed the little courtyard here he lived into an open-air cinema.

He mostly screened cartoons and comedies, featuring beloved acts ꞔe Laurel and Hardy and the clown Ridolini.

Bepi had a gruff but likeable personality and was affectionately ıown by two nicknames: *Bepi delle caramelle* ('Bepi of the Sweets') due his post-cinema candy-selling trade, and *Bepi Suà* ('Sweaty Bepi'), a ayful nod to his habit of working tirelessly under the summer sun, ten in sweat-soaked vests.

Far from being offended, ɜpi embraced this mo-ker, even inscribing ʾasa de Bepi Suà' on the ɔorframe of his home.

Today, Bepi's house undoubtedly the most ıotographed in Burano.

Every inch, from the indowsills to the TV ıtennas, is painted in ·ight hues, with the ıcade adorned in striking ɔometric patterns.

It's a colourful homage to quirky and unforgettable ıaracter.

BELL TOWER OF SAN MICHELE ARCANGELO DI MAZZORBO

A lonely bell tower, without a church

Isola di Mazzorbo
Vaporetto: line 12

Standing alone within a vineyard at the northernmost part of the island of Mazzorbo, the 27-metre-tall San Michele Arcangelo Bell ower, also known as the 'Angel's Bell Tower', is a striking sight.

Built in a Romanesque Renaissance style, the tower is made entirely exposed brick. In the bell chamber, only one of the four original bells mains: two others can still be found on Mazzorbo at the Church of nta Caterina, while the whereabouts of the fourth is unknown.

The accompanying church, constructed in the 11th century, was emolished during the Napoleonic era.

In its place, an oratory was built, serving a cemetery that, under e Saint-Cloud Edict (which banned burials in churches for hygiene asons and required them to take place away from inhabited areas), ecame the final resting place for the deceased from the islands of urano, Mazzorbo and Torcello.

Today, the cemetery no longer exists, having been replaced by a small ark.

A significant restoration of the bell tower was completed in 2024. ans for the future include opening the structure to the public, allowing sitors to ascend to the bell chamber and enjoy the panoramic views.

THE ORIGINAL CLAPPERS OF THE BELLS OF THE CHURCH OF SANTA CATERINA DI MAZZORBO

Europe's oldest bell

Fondamenta di Santa Caterina, 54
Vaporetto: line 12

Many may be surprised to learn that one of the islands in the Venetian Lagoon is home to what is considered the oldest bell in ırope, dating to 1318.

This remarkable bell is housed in the tower of the Church of Santa ıterina on Mazzorbo. Originally, it was in the bell tower of San ichele Arcangelo, also on Mazzorbo, before being moved to its current cation in 1819, when Santa Caterina was elevated to the status of a rish church.

The bell's unique alloy – created by fusing bronze, gold and silver – ıs believed to have the power to ward off storms.

According to an ancient popular belief, its sound waves disrupt the agnetic fields in the atmosphere, reducing the intensity of lightning rikes and decreasing the likelihood of them discharging in the mediate area.

The bell is adorned with a depiction of the Archangel Michael, the scription *MAGISTER LUCAS DE VENETIIS ME FECIT* ('Master ıcas of Venice made me') above the date, and the phrase *Xus vincit Xus gnat Xus imperat* ('Christ conquers, Christ reigns, Christ rules') below.

Beside it hangs another bell, dating to 1567 and also relocated from e Angel's Bell Tower, along with a smaller third bell, likely used as a gnal for liturgical functions.

The bell chamber is not accessible to the public. The original ıppers of the bells are now preserved and displayed in the church oister, housed in a dedicated che. These clappers were oved after the mechanism ıs electrified in 1986.

Historical records indicate at Santa Caterina's bell wer once held four bells, detailed in documents ferring to repairs to the wer.

By 1808, only three mained, which were ctioned off that same year Antonio Pigazzi.

TOMBSTONE OF FRANGOLA GIUSTINIAN

An upside-down face

Island of San Francesco del Deserto
The convent is accessible only by guided tour, every day except Monday or occasional days at the fraternity's discretion, with departures at the following times: 9am; 9.45am; 10.30am; 3pm; 3.45pm; 4.30pm
Punctuality is required to ensure every visitor has a good experience
The tour of the cloister, church and part of the garden, led by a friar, lasts abo[ut] 40 minutes
Booking is required for groups
Reservations are not accepted more than two months before the chosen date
The visit is free, but a voluntary donation is appreciated to support the island['s] maintenance
You can reach San Francesco del Deserto by private boat, water taxi or by public transport to Burano; from there, as there's no public transport to San Francesco del Deserto, you can contact Laguna Fla Group (Massimiliano 03479 922 959)

Next to the church of San Francesco del Deserto stands a chapel dedicated to the Madonna. There's also a small oratory, separated om the chapel by a window with a sill that conceals a truly curious ature – one that can only be seen reflected. It's only by using a mirror at a woman's face is revealed, that of Frangola Giustinian, whose stone mbstone was placed upside down as fill material to create the small lcony.

The lower part of the tombstone, found in the convent's garden, was aced in the chapel only in recent years d shows the woman depicted wearing e Franciscan habit and cord.

Frangola Giustinian, a tertiary of the anciscan Order, financed the renovation the church in 1401, whose roof has the aracteristic shape of a ship's hull.

Her remains, along with other bones scovered during various works, rest here she requested, in front of the urch.

Between the chapel dedicated to the Madonna and the church of San Francesco stands the oratory of the same name, a place which, according to tradition, was built by the Saint of Assisi himself. Today it houses the statue of Francis receiving the stigmata.

Not even the Convent of San Francesco was immune to the Napoleonic suppressions: the island became a military barracks, the buildings were adapted for this purpose, and the garden and meadow were rented out.

The convent was restored to the Franciscans only on 23 December 1856. The damage was extensive, and substantial restoration was needed to rehabilitate the buildings.

The original bells, removed during the French occupation, were replaced by bells from the church of Santa Lucia, which was demolished in 1861 to make way for the railway station.

Today one of these bells can be seen in the cloister. It bears the year 1753 as its casting date and the inscription *Opus Eredum De Poli*, which identifies the maker as the famous De Poli Foundry. This was one of the oldest foundries in Italy, with a documented presence in Venice throughout the 18th century.

Pan e Vin on Sant'Erasmo: a purifying ritual and an omen for the year ahead

On some of the lagoon islands, particularly where rural traditions are still alive, a time-honoured ritual takes place on the night of 5 January, or sometimes on the evening of Epiphany (6 January): the burning of the Pan e Vin bonfire.

The tradition of reading the sparks from Epiphany fires is a deeply rooted custom in the countryside of northern Italy, and it lives on in the Venetian Lagoon too – especially on the island of Sant'Erasmo, also known as 'the Doges' vegetable garden', where the Pan e Vin gathering attracts a large crowd each year.

The direction of the sparks is interpreted as a sign of how the new year will unfold.

A local saying goes: *Pan e vin, la pinsa soto el camin. Faive a ponente panoce gnente, faive a levante panoce tante* ('Bread and wine, the pinza under the hearth. Sparks to the west, no corn cobs; sparks to the east, plenty of corn').

The verse also mentions pinza, a rustic cake made from traditional ingredients common in rural households: white and yellow flour, yeast, sugar, milk, pine nuts, dried figs, raisins, fennel seeds and a splash of grappa.

This seasonal treat is typically shared among the community gathered around the fire, often accompanied by *vin bulè* ('mulled wine').

The symbolism attached to this custom is rich and meaningful. Like many fire-related traditions, Pan e Vin has ancient pre-Christian roots as a ritual of purification and good fortune.

The name itself – meaning 'bread and wine' – was likely chosen to evoke prosperity and abundance, although the name and details vary by location.

Still today, the bonfire represents the desire to burn away the old and look ahead to the new with hope.

Traditionally, the fire is lit with a piece of nadalin, the log burned in the hearth on Christmas Eve.

In some villages, the fire is blessed, and the crackling of holy water sprinkled onto the flames by the priest is thought to drive away evil spirits.

As well as the one on Sant'Erasmo, another Pan e Vin worth noting takes place on the evening of 6 January on the Lido of Venice, in the historic village of Malamocco, in the area known as Canadà.

PAINTING OF THE MARTYRDOM OF SAINT ERASMUS

A fascinating work attributed to Tintoretto's school

Church of Christ the King
Island of Sant'Erasmo
Via de le Motte, 110
041 5229418
Vaporetto: line 13

Built in 1929 to a design by architect Brenno Del Giudice, the church dedicated to Christ the King on Sant'Erasmo houses a fascinating painting attributed to the school of Jacopo Tintoretto, depicting the martyrdom of Saint Erasmus.

The martyrdom is portrayed in a highly theatrical manner: at the centre of the scene is Saint Erasmus, whose intestines are being torn out with a specialised device. As patron saint of sailors, Saint Erasmus began to be depicted with a windlass, a tool used for raising anchors.

Popular tradition gradually transformed this into an instrument of martyrdom, creating a horrific torture that became his classic visual representation.

Several onlookers witness the gruesome scene, some with expressions of horror, others showing compassion and pity. To the right is a glimpse of a hilly landscape with a fortified building, which sets the scene in an outdoor environment.

Why is Saint Erasmus the protector of seafarers?

Saint Erasmus is the protector of seafarers because, according to legend, after being saved from a shipwreck, he promised the captain to warn him of storms with fires, as a sign of his divine power.

The saint kept his promise, appearing with bluish flames that warned of approaching storms, protecting other ships as well.

This is why sailors pray to Saint Erasmus during storms. He is associated with a weather phenomenon called 'Saint Elmo's Fire' (another name by which he is known).

This electrical discharge happens when the air becomes ionised during storms at sea, creating a blue light that appears on the tips of ship masts.

CIRCULAR OPENING OF THE TORRE MASSIMILIANA

14

The only military construction of its kind remaining in Italy

Island of Sant'Erasmo
Ridotto Sant'Erasmo Nuovo, località Punta Vela
Via dei Forti s.n.c
Open in May during the Violet Artichoke Festival and for art exhibitions
Vaporetto: line 13

Anyone passing along the eastern side of the island of Sant'Erasmo can't help but notice the Torre Massimiliana, a curious, circular fortress inspired by defensive concepts dating back five centuries.

Once through the entrance, look up and you'll be struck by the unusual view of the sky glimpsed through a circular opening above the building's central block.

You can reach the structure's highest point via a spiral staircase leading to a terrace offering an enchanting 360-degree view.

The multi-storey building follows the design of so-called Martello towers – circular fortresses that take their name from the 16th-century Torre della Mortella in Corsica. These structures were erected at strategic points along the Corsican coast to protect coastal villages and maritime traffic from pirates. Later, other armies built similar constructions in locations near the sea – you can find them along the English Channel, for instance. It was the British who recognised their military effectiveness and changed the name from Mortella to Martello.

The Sant'Erasmo tower, built by the Austrians between 1843 and 1844, was named Massimiliana in honour of Emperor Maximilian, who commissioned it.

The building stands on the site of the earlier Fort Sant'Erasmo erected by the French from 1811–14. Surrounded by a water-filled moat and an irregular embankment, it defended the southern part of the coastline, while other structures called Ridotti Sant'Erasmo Vecchio and Nuovo were positioned to the north-east, forming a defensive system facing the Lido harbour entrance.

Of these defensive works, what remains today are the Torre Massimiliana itself and the blockhouse of Sant'Erasmo Nuovo, while telemetric towers have been built in place of the other fortifications.

The Sant'Erasmo Martello tower is the only one of its kind in Italy.

During the Second World War, it was used as an anti-aircraft battery. After years of neglect, it has since been restored.

Today it hosts art exhibitions and cultural events.

A tower that served as housing for several families

After the war, the Torre Massimiliana housed around 10 homeless families, who settled and lived here until relatively recent times. The rental contracts are preserved in the General Archives of the City of Venice.

POWDER MAGAZINES OF THE LAZZARETTO NUOVO

16

The Republic's historic gunpowder magazines

Island of Lazzaretto Nuovo
lazzarettiveneziani.it
Visits by appointment only
Vaporetto: line 13

On the island of Lazzaretto Nuovo, two buildings – set within the fortified walls but at some distance from the Tezon Grande – stand out from the rest. Enclosed by their own perimeter fences, they sit on pale Istrian stone foundations rather than the usual brick. These are the *caselli da polvere*, or powder magazines: buildings designed to store explosives.

Originally constructed entirely in Istrian stone, the magazines featured sharply pointed roofs designed to contain the force of any accidental explosion. Unlike the rest of the island, which was managed by the Magistrato alla Sanità (Health Magistracy), these structures fell under the jurisdiction of the Magistrato alle Artiglierie (Artillery Magistracy). For added security, the powder magazines were kept under dual lock and key, with one held by the Patron and the other by the Massaro (administrator) of the Venetian Arsenal.

In the second half of the 16th century, the Venetian Senate decided to decentralise the main Arsenal's explosive storage following a series of devastating fires – most notably the blaze of 1509, recorded by Marin Sanudo in his *Diarii*, and another in 1569.

The powder stores were relocated to various islands, including Certosa and the Fort of San Felice in Chioggia. During the Napoleonic occupation and under Austrian rule, the island retained its military role. It was even connected by tracks to the island of Sant'Erasmo and the Maximilian Tower. The powder magazines, as we see them today, reflect 19th-century alterations. Restored in the 1990s, they retain much of their original architectural character. For years, the larger of the two buildings hosted educational exhibitions which have now been transferred to the Tezon Grande.

PATH OF THE BARENE

17

A scenic walk along an ancient patrol path in the world's first quarantine station

Island of Lazzaretto Nuovo
Vaporetto: line 13
Visits by appointment only
lazzarettiveneziani.it

At the entrance to the Venetian Lagoon, the island of Lazzaretto Nuovo has held a strategic role since ancient times, guarding the waterways leading inland.

Today, visitors can follow the Sentiero delle Barene, a scenic nature trail established in 1992 that retraces the old patrol route once used by sentries. Along the way, a series of interpretive panels shed light on the lagoon landscape and its ecological richness.

The path leads past centuries-old mulberry trees, planted during the period of Austrian rule, and arrives at the Tezon Grande (see following double page), one of the island's key landmarks. The fortified walls dating from the 19th century are still intact.

A large, open meadow within the walls reveals the remains of ancient structures recently brought to light through excavation, including the small Church of San Bartolomeo and the former prior's residence. Just outside the walls is the cemetery, which has also been the focus of recent archaeological investigation.

The island also features a wellhead, likely once located within the riory grounds but later moved and reused atop an Austrian-era cistern. s bas-relief carving of the moeca lion (the winged lion of Venice) dates the late 15th or early 16th century and has remarkably survived the ontoclasty –the systematic destruction of Venetian symbols carried ut during the Napoleonic occupation. In the Middle Ages, the island as home to a Benedictine monastery and a church dedicated to San artolomeo, and was then known as the Vigna Murada (Walled Vineyard).

In the second half of the 15th century, a decree by the Senate of the erenissima Republic transformed the island into a lazaretto, not for reating plague victims – as was the case on nearby Lazzaretto Vecchio – ut for preventative quarantine. Crews, passengers and cargo arriving in enice were held there temporarily to stop the spread of disease.

Goods were isolated and subjected to strict controls, often fumigated ith aromatic herbs like juniper and rosemary. According to historical ecords, this is the first known instance in the world of such quarantine rocedures being formally carried out.

To house people in quarantine, around one hundred small houses ere built along the island's perimeter. The Venetian-style chimneys ound throughout the numerous rooms gave the place the vague ppearance of a castle.

By the 18th century, the island's health-related role had faded, and uring the Napoleonic and later Austrian occupations it was repurposed or military use.

TEZON GRANDE OF LAZZARETTO NUOVO

14

The second largest public building in the lagoon after the Arsenal's ropewalks

Island of Lazzaretto Nuovo
Vaporetto: line 13
Visits by appointment only
lazzarettiveneziani.it

The Tezon Grande (also known as Tezon Grando or Tezzone) was built around 1561–62, most likely replacing an earlier timber ructure. Measuring an impressive 102 by 22 metres, it is the largest ublic building in Venice after the Corderie (rope-making halls) of the rsenale.

Originally conceived as a long colonnaded portico with 60 arches, e building served to air out goods arriving on the island. These were id out under the cover of a vast roof to protect them from the rain. 's thought that a raised walkway once ran along the interior walls, lowing guards to supervise the process from above.

Various methods were used for disinfection: in addition to fumigation ith aromatic herbs, goods were exposed to open air, seawater or boiling ater, as well as to vinegar and ash.

In the 19th century, the Tezon was repurposed as a powder magazine, move that ultimately spared it from demolition. The original arcades ere walled up using materials salvaged from other demolished ructures on the island. To reinforce the building, buttressing pillars ere added against the central wall, and the terracotta floor was covered ith wooden planks.

Today, the building is divided into two sections. One houses a museum stallation showcasing e island's archaeological nds alongside traditional oats and tools once used y local craftsmen.

The other part serves a storage facility for rchaeological material covered from across the goon. These artefacts will ventually go on display in e forthcoming National rchaeological Museum f the Venetian Lagoon, ut for now, this section mains closed to the ublic.

GRAFFITI OF THE TEZON GRANDE, LAZZARETTO NUOVO

Striking traces left by quarantined crews

Island of Lazzaretto Nuovo
lazzarettiveneziani.it
Visits by appointment only
Vaporetto: line 13

Along the walls and pillars of the Tezon Grande, you'll find a wealth of historic graffiti – drawings and inscriptions made over ıe centuries by sailors, merchants and workers who passed through ıe island. These include merchant monograms, trademarks, crosses, .epictions of sea voyages and even references to historical events.

Made using a mixture of crushed brick and casein, the graffiti were ·nly discovered by chance in the 1980s after a section of the roof ollapsed. Rainwater seeped in and dissolved the layers of limewash that ıad long covered the walls, revealing inscriptions that serve as valuable vidence of the people who lived and worked there. They now stand as a ıistorical record of linguistic and anthropological significance.

Among these traces are signs of everyday life, markings of passage, .ecorative elements, commercial symbols and coats of arms. At the ·ezon Grande, the graffiti form a vivid historical record – offering nsight into the activities once carried out here and the origins of those vho passed through.

Many of the markings are directly tied to the building's function: the .iring and fumigation of ships' cargo. To avoid confusion among the ;oods laid out for disinfection, workers would reproduce the trademarks nd seals directly on the walls and pillars.

Alongside these practical inscriptions, others are of a different nature: eligious symbols, drawings of people and ships, decorative flourishes nd written notes that recount specific events. One notable example s a message from Antonio Trevisan, who recorded his presence at .azzaretto Nuovo from 6 July to the end of August 1585. He was with ıis team of bastazi (porters) to disinfect cargo from a ship arriving from Constantinople. He notes the death of Doge Nicolò Da Ponte and the ·lection of his successor, Pasquale Cicogna, concluding with the phrase: Long live the good comrades.'

Other written testimonies were eft by porters, giving the day, nonth and year of their arrival ɔn Lazzaretto Nuovo to disinfect ;oods. Some inscriptions also show vhere people came from, which n the 16th century was mostly rom the province of Brescia. All he inscriptions are written in the ·ernacular, with strong Venetian nfluences: some are carved within lecorative toothed frames, others ıre free-standing.

BONES IN THE DUOMO OF MURANO

Part of a whale's backbone

Basilica of Saints Mary and Donatus in Murano
sandonatomurano.it
Opening hours available on the website
Vaporetto: lines 3, 4.1 and 4.2

Behind the high altar of the Basilica of Saints Mary and Donatus in Murano – one of the finest examples of Veneto–Byzantine architecture in the entire Lagoon – you'll see a set of enormous bones hanging beneath the apse mosaic of the Virgin Orans. According to legend, these are the bones of a large and fearsome dragon defeated by St Donatus, Bishop of Evorea, with a simple sign of the cross.

What are supposedly the ribs and enormous tooth of the dragon slain by the saint are actually three ribs and part of a whale's backbone.

Dating from the 7th century, the building was originally dedicated to St Mary, but when the saint's body was brought from Cephalonia in 1125, the church was rededicated to both St Mary and St Donatus.

Work on rebuilding the original structure and bell tower also began at this time. It remains the oldest place of worship on Murano, and a keen observer will spot some ancient Roman artefacts at the base of its facade, probably brought from Altinum.

The mosaic floor, made of marble and glass paste, dates from the 12th century and is therefore contemporary with that of St Mark's Basilica – a fact recorded in an inscription within a circle, part of a geometric design representing the 'Ascension of Christ into Heaven'.

The iconography is complex: animal and plant motifs linked to biblical references form beautiful geometric patterns.

Donatus isn't the only saint in the Venetian area to have dealt with a dragon. Other dragon-slaying saints include St George, St Margaret and St Theodore (Todaro).
Of course, dragons didn't exist. Symbolically, slaying a dragon meant eliminating evil from human hearts or, in some cases, represented the defeat of Muslims by Christians.

TRACES OF ALTINUM IN THE BAPTISTERY OF THE DUOMO OF MURANO

20

Remnants of a city abandoned in the 7th century

Basilica of Saints Mary and Donatus in Murano
info@sandonatomurano.it - sandonatomurano.it
Opening hours available on the website
Vaporetto: lines 3, 4.1 and 4.2

You'll notice the presence of some interesting artefacts from the city of Altinum (see below), reused as decorative or liturgical elements, both outside and inside the Basilica of Saints Mary and Donatus in Murano.

One notable example is the funerary monument of the decurion Lucius Acilius, which was broken up and repurposed. Two halves of the octagonal altar stand on either side of the basilica's door, while the chest-shaped urn was converted into a baptismal font and now stands to the right of the entrance.

Inside the baptismal font, you'll notice a striking polychrome glasswork in shades of yellow and green, created around 1970 by master glassmaker Luciano Vistosi (1931–2010), whose workshop was very close to the basilica.

On the sides you can read a Latin inscription specifying that Lucius Acilius, a member of the local senate, had a tomb made for himself and his relatives.

Meanwhile, in the central nave, there's an octagonal altar in Aurisina limestone decorated with plant shoots and tendrils, now serving as the base for a holy-water stoup.

Ancient Altinum

Ancient Altinum was a large Roman city (see p. 48) that housed the main Adriatic port of the Veneti. Located about 10 kilometres north of present-day Venice Airport, it was definitively abandoned by its inhabitants around the early decades of the 7th century and soon became an open-air quarry from which building materials were taken (see p. 53). The first studies of these reused Roman monuments began in the 15th century, when scholars started cataloguing the ancient stones and inscriptions incorporated into Venice's churches, palaces and houses. During the 19th century, many of these artefacts were removed from the buildings where they'd been installed and transferred to the Patriarchal Seminary of Venice, where they remain. However, many inscriptions, stones and marble fragments from Altinum can still be seen in their original locations throughout Venice and Murano.

CHOIR STALLS FROM THE CHURCH OF SAN GIOVANNI BATTISTA

2

A remarkable work in wood

Parish museum of San Pietro Martire – Campiello Marco Michieli, 5 – Murano
041 739704
Monday to Friday 10am–4pm
Vaporetto: Lines 3, 4.1, 4.2, 12

The sacristy of the Church of San Pietro Martire in Murano houses a remarkable wooden work dating from between 1664 nd 1672, created by the wood carver Pietro Morando, who worked ongside his father Paolo. Although payment receipts from the Scuola ever mention Paolo, it's almost impossible to believe that such a vast nd iconographically complex work – not to mention one of such xtraordinary visual impact – could have been created by a single person.

The choir stalls originally stood in the Church of San Giovanni attista, and were part of a large and important complex comprising a onvent, church and hospital.

Nothing remains of the complex today. After the Napoleonic pheavals that affected the area, all the buildings began to be destroyed om 1837 onwards. First they were converted into food and military upply warehouses and cattle stalls, then demolished entirely.

Fortunately, after the Napoleonic dissolution of religious houses, the arish priest Don Stefano Tosi bought some of the Confraternity's sacred rnishings, including the choir stalls. The 20 wooden panels depicting pisodes from the life of St John the Baptist, flanked by telamones, legorical figures, philosophers and emperors, were moved and adapted their new space by the *arangon* ('carpenter' in ialect), Gigi Bortoluzzi. He ost likely couldn't maintain e original arrangement due lack of space.

The Scuola's receipts ecord nine other carved atues with their decorations, which sadly no longer urvive.

Do take some time to bserve these works closely: the anatomical and aturalistic rendering is extraordinary; the figures seem to ome alive, characterised by etails studied down to the mallest element.

PALA DEI BARCAROLI

2

An important artwork from the Island of San Cristoforo della Pace

Parish museum of San Pietro Martire
Campiello Marco Michieli, 5
Murano
041 739704
Monday to Friday 10am–4pm
Vaporetto: lines 3, 4.1, 4.2, 12

There is one painting that stands out among the works in the paris museum of San Pietro Martire in Murano: the so-called *Pala d Barcaroli*, painted by Giovanni Agostino da Lodi and depicting th Nativity of Mary.

At the feet of the enthroned Virgin sits an angel playing music on marble pedestal, upon which the figure of St Christopher is painted ı chiaroscuro within a roundel. To her right stand St George and a ishop; to her left, St John the Baptist and another bishop.

This is a significant altarpiece, considered the first work in the lagoon ɔ show strong influences from Leonardo da Vinci's style; the artist had :udied under the master in Milan and was a great admirer of his work.

Interestingly, this painting comes from the island of San Cristoforo, vhich was joined to the island of San Michele in the first half of the 9th century (1835–39) to create Venice's new cemetery.

The Confraternity of the *Barcaroli* (ferrymen) of Murano was also onnected to San Cristoforo, and had an altar in the church dedicated ɔ the patron saint of ferrymen. Agostino da Lodi's altarpiece hung bove this altar.

The church that housed this work was razed to the ground and its rtistic treasures – including works by Cima da Conegliano, the Vivarini amily and a painting from Tintoretto's school – were scattered.

One work by Jacopo Bassano travelled particularly far. His *St Christopher with the Christ Child on his Shoulder* now resides in Havana's Museo Nacional de Bellas Artes in Cuba.

EMILIANI CHAPEL

2

An evocative place of prayer since the 16th century

Island of San Michele
Visible from the Church of San Michele
Cemetery: 7.30am–4.30pm (winter hours), 7.30am–6pm (summer hours)
Vaporetto: lines 4.1 – 4.2

On the island of San Michele, built against the main church, stands a striking chapel that can be entered from within the church or through its main entrance outside.

This is the Emiliani Chapel. The noblewoman Margherita Vitturi commissioned it in her 1427 will, leaving a substantial sum to the Procurators of St Mark's to build a place of worship dedicated to Santa Maria Annunziata, in memory of her husband Giambattista Emiliani.

The chapel was built between 1528 and 1543 to designs by the architect Guglielmo de' Grigi.

The hexagonal building is crowned by a white dome in Istrian stone and is a fine example of Venetian Renaissance architecture.

It houses three altars, each decorated with marble representations of the Annunciation, the Adoration of the Magi, and the Adoration of the Shepherds, all created by Giovanni Battista da Carona.

Outside, in niches on the chapel's exterior, you'll find large Istrian stone statues of St Margaret and St John the Baptist, also by Giovanni Battista da Carona.

Votive bridge from Fondamente Nove to the island of San Michele

For many years, the island of San Michele was connected to the city during the period of Commemoration of the Dead by a bridge of boats, breaking its evocative isolation for a few days.

Every year, crowds of Venetians (and others) would walk across this votive bridge, which ran from the Fondamente Nove, near Palazzo Donà delle Rose, to the cemetery's most famous entrance: the Stucky Gate.

There are photographic and artistic records of this makeshift bridge, such as the etching by Fabio Mauroner that can be found at Ca' Pesaro, or the celebrated painting by Italico Brass, visible at the International Gallery of Modern Art in Rome.

Newspaper reports are also rich in anecdotes: in 1901 the bridge was closed due to strong winds and a rowboat crashed into it. In 1902, an exceptionally large crowd wanted to reach the cemetery so, from the early morning, men were forced to make way for women and children. In 1907, due to the cold and damp, one Venetian even fell into the water.
The tradition of erecting this bridge ended after 1950 and, for 69 years, the island of San Michele was no longer connected to the Fondamente Nove.
In 2019, the installation of a 407-metre long votive walkway allowed people to reach the cemetery more easily and also created an ideal link between present and past.
After an interruption of several years, partly due to the pandemic, the bridge was installed again in 2025.

UNUSUAL FACES IN THE CHURCH OF SAN MICHELE IN ISOLA

2

The mysterious faces carved on the barco *columns*

Cemetery: 7.30am–4.30pm (winter hours), 7.30am–6pm (summer hours)
Vaporetto: lines 4.1 – 4.2

nside the church of San Michele is a particular area reserved for the clergy, a structure once commonly used in Venice: a *barco*, or raised hoir gallery supported by pillars.

Few examples of these remain in the lagoon city, nearly all built etween the 15th and 16th centuries, and they can be seen in the hurches of San Sebastiano, Sant'Alvise and Santa Maria dei Miracoli.

On the arches supporting the barco are 10 highly detailed busts arved in bas-relief, which are genuine portraits: faces shrouded in a ertain mystery. In fact, it's still unclear whether these figures are purely ecorative or whether they represent craftsmen who worked at San Aichele during the building's construction, or perhaps some prominent gures from the monastery.

CHAPEL OF SAN CRISTOFORO

A beautiful space dedicated to an island that no longer exists

Cemetery of San Michele in Isola
Cemetery: 7.30am–4.30pm (winter), 7.30am–6pm (summer)
Vaporetto: lines 4.1– 4.2

Just a few steps from the hemicycle and the military and clergy sections on the island of San Michele stands the beautiful chapel f St Christopher.

Step inside and you'll be surprised by the beauty that suddenly nfolds; look up and the stunning mosaics within the octagonal dome eate a striking play of colour.

The church was built to commemorate the 'vanished island' of San ristoforo. Architect Giannantonio Selva was commissioned to build a nall temple (or oratory) on the site where the previous church stood efore its demolition.

The original plans called for a circular building with a domed roof, cluding a series of porticos with arches designed to house funerary ıonuments.

However, lack of funds forced the project to be scaled back. Selva uilt an octagonal chapel instead, with two entrances shaped like enotaphs.

Construction took around two years. The chapel was blessed on 28 ıne 1813 by the Bishop of Faenza, Monsignor Stefano Bonsignore, ho was serving as acting administrator of Venice's patriarchal see at ıe time.

After restoration, the altar inside has been dedicated to the memory f St Pius X (Cardinal Giuseppe Sarto, who served as Patriarch of enice from 1893 to 1903). At the chapel's centre, a mosaic by master aftsman Cesare Castaman reproduces Giovanni Bellini's celebrated ainting of St Christopher.

Since 1891, Venice has granted the chapel in perpetual use to ıe Archconfraternity and Company of San Cristoforo and della lisericordia. For around two centuries, this organisation has ccompanied the deceased to burial and now also provides volunteer ıpport for elderly people in need.

As is well known, the cemetery of San Michele in Isola was created by joining two islands: Saints Honorius and Christopher of the Peace, and San Michele. They were unified in the first half of the 19th century specifically to establish the new cemetery.

CHURCH OF SANT'EUROSIA

Why does Eurosia protect us during storms?

Island of Vignole
Sunday 9.30am–10.30am (open for Sunday Mass)
Vaporetto: line 13

On the green island of Vignole, once washed directly by the sea an formerly known as Biniola or Island of the Seven Vineyards, the is a small church dedicated to St Mary of the Assumption, but know locally as the little church of Sant'Eurosia, a patron saint of harvests an protector from storms, drought and floods.

On an island where the few inhabitants still live by working th fields, devotion to a saint who protects from storms makes perfe

:nse: just one heavy downpour or storm could ruin months of work ıd make the harvest unusable.

The story of Eurosia is remarkable. As an orphan, she was taken in y the rulers of Bohemia, who raised her as their own daughter and onverted her to Christianity.

When Pope John VIII needed to find a bride for the son of the ount of Aragon, Saint Methodius recommended the young woman. urosia began her journey to meet her future husband, but Saracens ıptured her in the mountains.

They demanded she give up her Christian faith, but when she :fused, they killed and beheaded her.

The moment she died, an incredible storm erupted with fierce inds, lightning and thunderous roars. A heavenly voice announced ıat Eurosia would now have the power to calm storms whenever people ılled on her name.

Spanish soldiers brought this saint's orship to Italy, first to the north, then the Veneto region through farmers om Treviso and Friuli, where her cult as already popular from the 1500s to 700s.

You can find many church bells cross Italy dedicated to Sant'Eurosia. armers would ring them to drive away :orms and hailstorms, continuing ncient agricultural traditions.

In the countryside, Venetian ırmers would leave their first seasonal rops as offerings at shrines dedicated this saint.

Within private property, this church-oratory is probably the only one still existing among the many that once stood on the lagoon islands. It reflects the popular devotion of rural character, on one of the few cultivable islands that still live by agriculture today.

A small curiosity is that the building doesn't have a baptismal font; when needed, one is specially brought from the Church of Christ the King on Sant'Erasmo.

SECRETS OF FORT SANT'ANDREA

The military masterpiece of architect Michele Sanmicheli

Accessible by private boat or, on Ascension Sunday only, by shuttle service fro
Venice Lido

If you love the history of the Venetian Republic or have a passion f military history and architecture, Fort Sant'Andrea is unmissable ar unique. It was built on the remains of a 15th-century tower and a outer bastion, which housed defensive gun batteries at its base.

The structure was created through collaboration between military ngineer Antonio da Castello and architect Michele Sanmicheli (or ammicheli) as part of efforts to strengthen the city's protective system.

Looking at the bastion, you'll notice the beautiful three-arch gateway, here only the central arch is open for entry, flanked by two others pped with grotesque masks and small openings for cannons.

Beyond its military function, the work was carefully designed om an aesthetic standpoint, as this was the first monument visitors ncountered when entering through the Port of San Nicolò.

The fort only fired once at an enemy vessel – against the French iip *Le Libérateur d'Italie* on 20 April 1797, killing the commander nd forcing the ship to surrender. Later, during French rule, the fort as strengthened, and in 1964 work was carried out to stop foundation ttlement.

During the First World War, Sant'Andrea island housed a Royal Navy aplane station. The island also has a small church (now deconsecrated) iat looks very similar to the one at the Lido's Ospedale al Mare, also edicated to Santa Maria Nascente.

The fort structure has recently undergone major restoration work. oday the island is for sale and the building has been extensively andalised.

Giacomo Casanova was imprisoned here from March to July 1743.

Even today, on the Festa della Sensa (Ascension Day), a procession of boats carrying the Mayor and other authorities goes to Sant'Andrea island to receive homage from a battalion of re-enactors dressed as 17th-century soldiers, lined up on the upper terrace.

A commemorative plaque for the battle of Lepanto

On the front of the tower is a commemorative plaque for the battle of Lepanto. It's topped by a relief showing the Lion of St Mark, while at the summit of the tower is a terrace.

The Festa della Sensa and the Fort of Sant'Andrea

Every year, on Ascension Sunday, the Fort of Sant'Andrea hosts a special occasion.

Shortly after the traditional and cherished 'Marriage of Venice to the Sea' – held in front of the Church of San Nicolò on the Lido – the ceremonial boat procession makes its way towards the fort to pay homage. A group of historical re-enactors in period dress gather on the terrace below the flagpole where the banner of Saint Mark flies.

The Festa della Sensa is an ancient celebration still held on the day of the Ascension. In the time of the Serenissima (the Most Serene Republic of Venice), it was one of the grandest and most emblematic of official festivities, followed by a lively fair that attracted more than 100,000 people during the eight (later 15) days of celebrations.

The Republic of Venice traced the origins of the event to the peace treaty of 1177, signed in Venice between Pope Alexander III and Emperor Frederick Barbarossa. In reality, Ascension Day had already been marked with solemn ceremonies before 1177 – likely in memory of Doge Pietro Orseolo II's departure on that very day in the year 1000, when he set sail to confront Adriatic pirates.

It is possible the Sensa festival has even older roots, descending from pre-Christian rituals for invoking favourable conditions, later absorbed into Christian tradition.

The day began with a solemn Mass in the Basilica of Saint Mark, followed by a grand dogal procession aboard the Bucintoro, the state barge, bound for the Lido. There, the Patriarch would bless the Doge and the lagoon waters.

A second blessing took place offshore at San Nicolò: the Doge would cast a gold ring into the sea while pronouncing the words, *Desponsamus te mare in signum veri perpetuique dominii* ('We wed thee, O sea, as a symbol of true and eternal dominion').

On this day, the Fort of Sant'Andrea opens its gates to the public. A dedicated shuttle service runs from the Lido (San Nicolò area) to the island of Sant'Andrea. The short crossing takes only a few minutes.

REMAINS OF THE CLOISTER OF SAN BRUNO

2

A 15th-century monastery

Island of Certosa
Vaporetto: lines 4.1 or 4.2 (request stop)

Walking around the island of Certosa, you can see what remain of a monastery cloister whose history began in 1422, whe Carthusian monks arrived from Florence. The island, previously know as Sant'Andrea del Lido (after a monastery dedicated to the patron sair of fishermen), soon became known as the island of San Bruno, or dell Certosa.

At the centre of the cloister stands a tree: a hackberry that gre spontaneously thanks to residual water from the well that onc stood here. Known as *spaccasassi* (stone-breaker) because it can pus through even the hardest surfaces, it became the focus of an art projec Between June 2023 and January 2024, the tree featured in one of fou installations bringing together artists, architects, designers, philosophe and botanists to explore the island's history and natural environment.

Seventeenth- and eighteenth-century engravings show Certosa a a green island where the monks' cells were arranged around a squa cloister. A smaller cloister was attached to the church.

There was also a boathouse, farmhouse and guesthouse for visitors. The complex was completed by a large vegetable garden and an extensive fish pond. The church, built after the Carthusians' arrival, was richly decorated and housed various tombs, including those of Doges Nicolò Marcello and Alvise Pisani.

Why did the Certosa of San Bruno take this name?

Born in Cologne in 1030, in 1084 Bruno travelled to the Chartreuse massif near Grenoble in the French Alps. He spent six years in a wild and remote 15,000-hectare estate where, with six companions, he founded the first monastery, which became the foundation of a contemplative order that still exists today. The name *Chartreuse* has been translated into various languages, including English (Charterhouse), Spanish (*Cartuja*) and Italian (*Certosa*).

The legend of the treasure

According to legend, treasure is buried here. It is said that when Napoleon arrived, the three senators in charge of the State Mint sought to protect all the gold by concealing it in the small cloister, though the story has no historical foundation. The monastery and church were suppressed in 1810, and everything was demolished and dispersed. No trace of the treasure has ever been found.

The violet artichoke of Sant'Erasmo: a unique flavour because it grows on sandy soil

Delicious to eat and beautiful to behold, the artichoke is actually the bud of a violet flower – *Cynara* (the Latin name that also inspired the famous artichoke-based liqueur). If left unharvested, it blooms into a striking thistle-like blossom. 'Violet' is also the name of the prized artichoke variety grown on Sant'Erasmo and the star of the popular festival held in its honour on the second Sunday of May.

Historical records show that artichokes were being cultivated in Venice as early as the 1500s, and the Austrian land registry of the early 19th century confirms the continuing importance of this celebrated crop. This particular variety belongs to the species *Cynara scolymus* and can be enjoyed in many different ways. The tender early shoots, known as *castraure*, are eaten raw, deep-fried in batter, braised in the Greek style, served cold with lemon, or paired with schie – small local grey shrimp.

Production is concentrated on the islands of Sant'Erasmo, Vignole and Mazzorbo, the Cavallino–Treporti peninsula, the lagoon's estuarine zones, and parts of the municipality of Chioggia – all within the province of Venice.

›YROTECHNICS CHIMNEY

29

The remains of munitions production during World War I

sland of Certosa
'aporetto: lines 4.1 or 4.2 (request stop)

n the heart of what is now the green lungs of Certosa, a towering chimney recalls a very different past. During World War I, the Italian overnment established a large, modern munitions factory on the sland – the Pirotecnica della Certosa – operated by the Royal Navy. The actory was closed in 1957 and completely decommissioned in 1962.

With its octagonal base, the masonry structure rises to around 18 netres and dominates the western part of the island known as Isola 'ecchia.

It's also worth noting that the military activity significantly altered the sland's shape. A new trapezoidal section, already visible in photographs rom the 1940s, was created using material excavated from the seaplane ase (*idroscalo*).

THE GUARDIAN

30

A powerful message of renewal

Island of Certosa
Vaporetto: Lines 4.1 or 4.2 (request stop)

The Guardian – that's the name given to this striking figure of a woman gazing out over the lagoon. It's a fitting title for a sculpture eated by Marco Martalar using reclaimed materials: wood, bark and ıutical ropes salvaged during the island's restoration.

The artist, already well known for his works made from debris left / the 2018 Vaia storm that struck the Dolomites and Venetian Prealps, gain conveys a profound message of rebirth and resilience.

The sculpture is impressive in scale, measuring 3 metres long, metres high, and 1.5 metres wide. It stands proudly on the side of the land facing the Lido of Venice, blending seamlessly into the lagoon ndscape.

Created in September 2020 in collaboration with several local sociations, the piece was built around a wooden framework to which e sculptor patiently attached each element, piece by piece, forming a ork of remarkable visual power.

After years of neglect, the island has had a remarkable revival. Since e early 2000s, renewed interest in its potential has transformed it into thriving nautical hub and a beautiful urban park in the heart of the enetian Lagoon.

N
San Michele
Le Vignole
Forte di Sant'Andrea
La Certosa
Aeroporto Giovanni Nicelli
Canale di San Nicolò
Riviera san Nicolò
Spiaggia libera di San Nicoletto
Ponte di Rialto
VENEZIA
Piazza San Marco
Spiaggia libera
Gran Viale Santa Maria Elisabetta
San Servolo
Lido
Canale Orfano
Via Sandro Gallo
Lungomare Guglielmo Marconi
Giudecca
San Lazzaro degli Armeni
Isola del Lido
Lazzaretto Vecchio
San Clemente
Santo Spirito
Sacca Sessola
Canale delle Scoazze
Canale di Santo Spirito
Mare Adriatico
Poveglia
Via Malamocco
Canale di Poveglia
Malamocco
Canale di Malamocco
Canale Campana
Via Alberoni
Fisolo
Canale Fisolo
Alberoni
Bacino di Malamocco
Faro Rocchetta
Spignon
0
500
1
2
3
4
5
6
7
8
9
10
11
12
13
14
15
16
17
18

Venice Lido

MILLSTONE ON RIVIERA SAN NICOLÒ

The mystery of the triskele

Riviera San Nicolò, in front of the church of the same name
Outdoors and always visible
Accessible by bus from Santa Maria Elisabetta Passenger Terminal: line A

On the waterfront opposite the Church of San Nicolò, close to th bus stop on the lagoon side, you'll find a large and mysteriou Istrian stone slab measuring 2.32 metres in diameter. At its centre is kind of *triskele* (see opposite page) – an ancient symbol formed by thre spirals joined at a central point.

It was discovered in 1995 along the San Nicolò waterfront durin building works, and its shape immediately suggested a millstone, theory also supported by old maps that confirm the presence of sever mills in the area.

According to another theory, proposed by the archaeologist in charg of the site where it was found, the circular form of the stone base migh suggest a different use. Perhaps it was used to channel liquids which through the central hole, were discharged into the conduit below.

However, the millstone theory remains the most widely accepted.

The symbolism of the triskelion: Europe's equivalent of the swastika?

The *triquetra* (from the Latin meaning 'three corners') or *triskelion* (from the Greek meaning 'three legs') is a symbol made up of three interlaced arcs, forming a continuous figure without a beginning or end.
A universal symbol linking different beliefs and traditions across the ages, the triskelion carries a profound meaning based on the idea of unity in diversity, the continuity of the life cycle, and protective power.
While the oldest representations are found in the megalithic temples of Malta, the motif is especially common in Celtic culture. There, the triskelion symbolises the trinity in its many forms: earth, air, and water or birth, life and death. It was often engraved on stones, jewellery, and weapons, embodying divine protection and eternity.
According to the archaeologist and historian Albert Grenier, among the Gauls it symbolised the sun, its movement representing the three visible phases of the day: morning, noon and twilight. It also represented the unity of Celtic society around three main castes: bards and druids (spiritual power), kings (temporal power) and peasants and craftsmen (material power), which mirrors the theoretical organisation of Hindu society.
In this way, the triskelion can be considered Europe's equivalent of the swastika, which has Hindu origins. Celtic religion, in fact, shares close metaphysical similarities with Hinduism.
The triskelion is also associated with the Celtic triple goddess (with figures like Brigid and the Morrigan), representing the three stages of a woman's life: maiden, mother and wise elder. Later, under Christian influence, it became a symbol of the Holy Trinity (Father, Son and Holy Spirit) and began to appear in religious art, particularly in illuminated manuscripts such as the *Book of Kells* (8th century).
Since 1285, the Sicilian flag has featured a triskelion: three legs radiating counterclockwise from a central human head. This design is called the *Trinacria*, after Sicily's three promontories that give the island its triangular shape.

RELIC OF SAN NICOLÒ

The remains of the patron saint of travellers and seafarers

Church of San Nicolò –Riviera S. Nicolò, 26
Lido di Venezia
Accessible every Sunday from 10am to 11.15am
Holy Mass: every Sunday at 11.30am
During the week the church may occasionally be open; it's advisable to call: 041 526 0241
Accessible by bus from Santa Maria Elisabetta Passenger Terminal: line A

Though it isn't widely known outside the local area, the Church of San Nicolò houses an urn containing a relic of great importance to Christian believers: half of St Nicholas's skeleton.

The sacred remains rest in an urn at the high altar, raised up beneath three statues depicting San Nicolò Magno, Bishop of Myra (to whom the church is dedicated), flanked by St Theodore, Bishop and Martyr, and San Nicolò Avunculo.

During the most recent examination of the relics in September 1992, the remains were confirmed as authentic and complementary to those in Bari, strengthening the theory that the original skeleton was divided.

This supports what the chronicles have recounted through the centuries: that the saint's remains were stolen by the people of Bari and the Venetians.

St Nicholas of Myra is one of the world's best-known saints, protector of travellers, seafarers and fishermen, patron saint of Russia, Greece and the city of Amsterdam, and – in Italy alone – of over 270 municipalities including, of course, Bari.

This part of the Lido has a long religious history. The present church dates from 1626–1629, but it replaced an earlier Byzantine structure built in 1053 that stood slightly further back. Excavations have revealed its remains, some of which are visible in the convent cloister.

The Church of San Nicolò hosts the Solemn Mass held each year on Ascension Day, the Festa della Sensa, after the ceremony of the Marriage of Venice to the Sea.

It's also a place of pilgrimage for Orthodox believers living in the city and surrounding area, as well as some tourists. Indeed, compared with the cathedral in Bari, this place remains relatively unknown to the masses, despite housing not only the saint's relics but several other fascinating

In Venice, St Nicholas is called *San Nicolò* and sometimes, though only in speech, *San Nicoletto*.

CHOIR OF THE CHURCH OF SAN NICOLÒ

③

A hidden Baroque masterpiece

Riviera S. Nicolò, 26
Lido di Venezia
Accessible every Sunday from 10am to 11.15am
Holy Mass: every Sunday at 11.30am
During the week the church may occasionally be open; it's advisable to call: 041 526 0241
Accessible by bus from Santa Maria Elisabetta Passenger Terminal: line A

Almost no one knows that in the apse of the church of San Nicolò there is a choir of extraordinary beauty. It is partly hidden by the imposing altar where the relics of St Nicholas rest and can be reached through a side passage near the sacristy.

Carved from walnut in a semicircular design, it was created in 1636 by Giovanni da Crema.

It features 27 stalls, each flanked by two Corinthian columns that frame a panel on which a significant episode from the life of St Nicholas is depicted in relief.

Each seat also has two armrests: the upper part features a cherub's head while the lower part displays a grotesque mask.

The crowning section presents a regular alternation of urns and finials.

Remarkably, the choir has survived nearly four centuries of alterations to the church.

A small relic of St Nicholas in the choir

At the back of the choir, at the foot of a statue of St Benedict, there's a casket containing an urn that holds a small relic of St Nicholas. This was taken from the saint's remains contained in the chest above the altar during the examination of 1992. It soon became an object of devotion and, since 2024, has been open to display the relics. The empty space inside the casket is constantly filled with the numerous notes containing prayers that the faithful leave for St Nicholas.

ANCIENT BELLS OF THE CHURCH OF SAN NICOLÒ 4

One of the rare relics of the famous Battle of Lepanto

Church of San Nicolò
Riviera S. Nicolò, 26
Lido di Venezia
Accessible every Sunday from 10am to 11.15am
Holy Mass: every Sunday at 11.30am
During the week the church may occasionally be open; it's advisable to call: 041 526 0241
Accessible by bus from Santa Maria Elisabetta Passenger Terminal: line A

Just inside the entrance to the Church of San Nicolò, on the left, you can see three bells up close, mounted on a wooden support measuring 4 metres by 1.5 metres, crafted by master shipwright Giuseppe Telaroli and marine engineer Luciano Girotto.

Cast in 1528, these bells are historically significant because they rang out in celebration on 18 October 1571 to announce the victory of the Holy League's ships over the Turkish fleet in the dramatic Battle of Lepanto, which took place in the Gulf of Corinth.

The naval battle was so big and bloody that it's considered the largest of the medieval and modern era in the Mediterranean, costing the lives of around 40,000 people.

Originally, the bells belonged to the old basilica of San Nicolò, where they remained until its demolition in 1622.

Once construction of the new church was completed in 1629, they were placed in the new bell tower, where they remained until 1937, when they were replaced by four new bells.

For over 70 years they were almost forgotten behind the high altar, in a barely visible space that didn't do justice to their historical importance.

In the 2000s, thanks to the initiative of Commander Ferruccio Falconi, they were restored and mounted on the wooden base where they stand today, in a space once occupied by an old confessional.

The installation was officially inaugurated on 5 December 2009.

UNKNOWN SYMBOLS OF THE OLD JEWISH CEMETERY OF THE LIDO

5

One of Europe's oldest surviving Jewish cemeteries

Via Cipro, 70 - Lido di Venezia
jvenice.org/cimitero-ebraico
Guided tours by appointment only
Accessible by bus from Santa Maria Elisabetta Passenger Terminal: line A

From outside, through the iron gate facing the lagoon (the ancien boundary of the burial ground), you can see part of the Old Jewisl Cemetery. However, to enter one of Europe's oldest surviving Jewisl cemeteries, you need to book ahead. Headstones jutting from unever ground, surrounded by tall trees and moss, create a deeply romantic atmosphere. This enchanted 19th-century Romantic poets and writer such as Goethe and Lord Byron during their stays in the city.

While many tombs display symbols found in Jewish cemeterie everywhere – such as the two raised hands in blessing, symbol of the Cohen family (see following double page) – other tombs feature les common symbols.

The harp, which appears on two headstones belonging to the ephardic Mugnon family, also marks the graves of those named Dawid)avid), referencing scriptures that describe the king as 'the sweet singer Israel'.

The cockerel (associated here with the Luzzatto family, whose ırname derives from the German region of Lausitz) awakens the eceased in preparation for resurrection and symbolises wisdom and vine providence.

You'll also encounter unique family symbols, such as the flying ınner of the Vivante family or the ladder supported by a lion elonging to the Sullam family. The ladder references the family name self: Sullam means 'ladder' in Hebrew. It also evokes the biblical story Jacob's ladder, symbolising the link between earth and heaven and iritual ascent.

Among the cemetery's most celebrated burials are two notable figures: lia Levita (1469–1549), a German poet and grammarian famous as the ıthor of *Bovo-Bukh*, the most popular chivalric romance in Yiddish, and eon da Modena (1571–1648), a rabbi, preacher and versatile scholar onsidered one of the most eminent figures in Italian Judaism.

It was in 1386 that the Republic of Venice allowed its Jewish ommunity to establish a cemetery on uncultivated land on the Lido, ear San Nicolò, despite protests from monks at the nearby monastery, ho claimed ownership. The cemetery became operational between 1386 ıd 1389, reaching its maximum size in 1641. It served as the main burial ace for Venetian Jews at least until the end of the 18th century.

One of the tombs depicts a Solomon's knot, see p. 150.

EARBY

he Modern Jewish Cemetery

ctober to March 9.30am–2.30pm and April to September 3pm–6.30pm
n Fridays and on the eve of Jewish holidays the cemetery closes at 2pm
losed Saturdays and Jewish holidays

ome 300 metres from the Old Jewish Cemetery stands the Modern wish Cemetery, in use since 1744. The move became necessary due to e deterioration of the old cemetery caused by erosion and structural ımage from military requisitions and troop occupation in the strategic ea near Fort San Nicolò. Notable burials here include important gures such as entrepreneur Michelangelo Jesurum, renowned for s polychrome lace – which won the Grand Prize at the 1878 Paris niversal Exhibition – and Isacco Pesaro Maurogonato, politician and nator of the Kingdom of Italy.

Symbols on Jewish tombstones

Symbols have always played a fundamental role in Judaism. Each graphic sign was assigned a characteristic or quality and was intended to represent the link between humankind and God (unlike diabolism, which separates humankind from God) and to identify a family or a religious function.

Tombstones in Jewish cemeteries feature some common themes, notably the 'priestly blessing', indicating the deceased person's priestly descent. This can be found on the tombstones of members of the Cohen (or Coen) family; in Hebrew *kohèn* means priest, i.e. a male descendent of Aaron, brother of Moses and first high priest of the Jewish community. The position of the hands, with spread fingers, is adopted during the blessing.

Another typical symbol is the pitcher pouring water. This symbol is a sign of belonging to the Israelite tribe of Levi (the Levi family), whose traditional duties were to assist priests during religious services by washing their hands before the blessing. The oldest tombstones also bear another symbol prominent in Jewish funerary symbolism: the crown. This represents both the political authority and the dignitary role of the deceased and comes from a quote from *Pirkei Avot* (*Ethics of Our Fathers*), one of the founding texts of Judaism: 'There are three crowns: the crown of Torah, the crown of priesthood and the crown of monarchy – but the crown of a good name outweighs them all.' From the 19th century, other symbols more in line with the trends

of the time began to appear. The *clepsydra* refers to the passage of time and the moment when life comes to an end. It sometimes bears wings, or can be associated with crossbones and a skull, making the connection to death even more evident. Similarly, the symbol of a torch turned upside down is used to represent mourning: the flame must be extinguished against the floor.

The *ouroboros*, the symbol of a serpent eating its own tail, recalls the notion of rebirth, while the crown of flowers can evoke the idea that the deceased acquired a reputation during his terrestrial life.

The butterfly, a symbol both ancient and common, refers to the soul departing the body and ascending into the sky.

The Star of David (*Magen David*) is perhaps the most famous symbol in Jewish culture. It was widely adopted throughout the 19th century and can be seen on many tombstones in cemeteries across the world.

Animal figures symbolise the name of the deceased: the lion, often seen next to a crown, not only indicates that the person is of royal descent and therefore belongs to David's lineage, it also refers to the name Leon (*Leo* in Italian, *Loeb* or *Loew* in Germany); the wolf is the emblem of Benjamin and is the representation of a very common surname in the Jewish community (*Wolf* in English and German, *Zeev* in Hebrew); and a deer, which represents descendants of the Naphtali tribe, refers to the surname *Hirsch* (in Yiddish and German), *Zvi* (in Hebrew) or *Naftali*.

Solomon's knot: A powerful symbol for binding and warding off spirits

Known by this name since ancient Rome and Greece, and used by master architects during the Middle Ages, Solomon's knot owes its name to Judaeo-Christian Kabbalah, which named it after the king who exchanged wealth for wisdom and reached true spiritual understanding.

If you look at Solomon's knot, you'll see two sets of threads weaving repeatedly through each other in constant geometry, forming a cross that loops back into itself with no beginning or end. This reflects the way in which humanity and the divine mirror each other, echoing the hermetic principle 'as above, so below'.

The story of the famous Gordian knot echoes this idea. Taking its name from the ancient city of Gordion (present-day Yassıhüyük) in central Anatolia, Turkey, this knot was believed to be impossible to untie, having neither beginning nor end, according to Plutarch. Legend held that whoever succeeded in untying it would become master of Asia.

Alexander the Great provided the solution by cutting through it with his sword. The legend tells that lightning and thunder struck the city that night as a sign of heavenly approval.

This episode marked a turning point in Alexander's conquest of Anatolia, granting him official consecration and divine lineage to claim the Phrygian kingdom – the starting point for extending his power across the region.

As their Greek and Roman predecessors, medieval architects used Solomon's knot to decorate temple and palace floors, walls and columns, binding higher forces to open the pathway of communication between earth and heaven through sacred ritual.

Popular belief extended the symbol to its apotropaic function (from the Greek *apotrépein*, meaning 'to ward off', 'to drive away evil'): for many, Solomon's knot is primarily considered a means of keeping evil at bay.

Magical ties or magic knots, like Solomon's knot, serve to catch and block spirits, whether good or evil. In popular culture, it was believed the Devil carried away lost souls, so they used magic knots to bind him, preventing his escape and stopping him from causing more harm.

As an eternal knot with no beginning or end, malevolent forces that venture into it follow endless lines and are trapped for eternity.

This explains the tradition of cursed places – sites where the Devil and evil spirits were believed to be trapped, held there by God's power, which was greater than their own.
Over time, Solomon's knot was gradually carved at entrances and inside homes as protection against malevolent influences.
Perhaps this also reflected a semi-forgotten habit dating back to Moses' time, when the Hebrews would paint their doorposts with lamb's blood so that God's plagues would not reach them.
Solomon's knot also appears in Islamic art. Some attribute this to the religious prohibition on figurative representations, others to the importance Muslims placed on studying mathematics and the science of numbers.
Still others see it as representing Allah's indivisibility and the mystical belief in the unity of humanity and God.

HOLES IN THE STONES OF THE NEW JEWISH CEMETERY

For marking boundaries

New Jewish Cemetery
Via Cipro, 70 - Lido di Venice
October to March 9.30am–2.30pm and April to September 3pm–6.30pm
On Fridays and on the eve of Jewish holidays the cemetery closes at 2pm
Closed Saturdays and Jewish holidays
Guided tours by appointment: jvenice.org/cimitero-ebraico
Accessible by bus from Santa Maria Elisabetta Passenger Terminal: line A

Just beyond the entrance to the New Jewish Cemetery, you'll find some rather unusual headstones that have circular holes in the lower sections, which were once embedded in the ground.

Numerous theories have been proposed about this feature, which was thought to have symbolic value: a kind of tunnel through which the soul of the deceased could reach the heavenly Jerusalem.

However, subsequent studies, along with comparisons to similar finds from Altinum, have instead led to the conclusion that these stones were previously used to mark boundaries and the perforated section was used to pass a pole through, providing greater stability to the rest of the stone block.

A tomb partly in the Catholic cemetery and partly in the New Jewish Cemetery

In the San Nicolò cemetery area, the tomb of Mario Friedenberg (1899–1969) is rather unusual: it's positioned half in the Catholic cemetery and half in the New Jewish Cemetery. Of Jewish faith, Friedenberg had married Egle Manara (1903–1983), who was Catholic.

Burials removed to make way for the Riviera San Nicolò roadway

In the Lapidarium, an inscription on a stele inside a small enclosure explains: 'Here rest the remains of 400 Jews whose burials (14th-18th centuries) were located until 1929 in the ancient cemetery along the lagoon'.

These are therefore burials that were removed to make way for the Riviera San Nicolò roadway.

The removal was especially painful for Venetian Jews for two reasons: it reduced the cemetery area and, more crucially, violated Jewish religious law, which forbids exhumation except when remains are transferred to Israel.

Since 1929, numerous headstones had lain stacked in the cemetery keeper's garden, and it was here that Commander Aldo Izzo felt compelled to give them a more dignified resting place. And so, in 2003, 139 headstones were cleaned and placed where they can now be admired and studied.

The hero who took his own life in 1943 rather than hand over the list of Jews living in Venice to the Nazis

In the New Jewish Cemetery lies the grave of Professor Giuseppe Jona, a man whose memory remains alive in Venice.

The tomb isn't easy to spot, but the cemetery keeper will be happy to point it out to anyone wishing to pay tribute to this true hero.

As well as being a distinguished anatomical pathologist at Venice's Ospedale Civile, he served as president of the Ateneo Veneto between 1921 and 1925 and, above all, was a person of exceptional humanity.

In Venice he was known as 'the doctor of the poor'. Despite being a celebrated medical luminary, Professor Jona treated countless people in financial hardship free of charge, often helping their families not only medically but financially.

He continued his philanthropic work even after the prohibitions imposed by the racial laws, often travelling at night as discreetly and anonymously as possible. To avoid being recognised he would wear a cloak and wide-brimmed hat.

In 1940, amid the turmoil of the Second World War, he accepted the leadership of Venice's Jewish community.

Though not particularly religious himself, he knew the times ahead would be especially difficult, probably even tragic. He was urged to leave Venice and hide in safer locations on multiple occasions. Someone had even offered to shelter him, and with his considerable wealth, he could easily have fled to Switzerland.

However, faithful to his enormous sense of responsibility, he refused to abandon Venice's Jewish community to its fate. In September 1943 the Nazis ordered him to hand over an updated list of the Jews remaining in the city.

Fearing he might give in under torture, he faced an extreme decision: he drew up a will donating most of his possessions to social and charitable causes. He also arranged for scholarships to be established at Venice's Ospedale Civile, to which he donated his medical library of 1,684 volumes, including rare books, some dating from the 16th century.

By now a hunted man, he first ensured that every document in his possession that could reveal the identity and addresses of Venetian Jews was hidden in a safe place. Then, on the evening of Thursday 16 September, he took his own life at his home at number 3826 Cannaregio, injecting himself with a lethal dose of morphine.

This act severely hindered deportation plans and represented a genuine rebuke to the Nazis, who banned any procession or display of affection at his funeral (which took place at the Ospedale Civile), imposing a maximum limit of 10 people at his burial on the morning of 19 September.
In Venice, round-ups of Jewish people began between 5 and 6 December, around three months later than in other cities. This delay resulted from Professor Jona's act, which made it particularly difficult to identify Jewish people still in the city.
This window of time that the professor managed to create through his sacrifice allowed many to seek refuge in the hinterland or even in Venice itself, in the homes of friends who courageously sheltered them at great personal risk.
It's impossible to know exactly how many people Professor Jona's sacrifice saved, but the number was certainly substantial – well over a thousand.

From the post-war period onwards, the city of Venice paid tribute with its admiration, esteem and gratitude to Professor Giuseppe Jona. One of the main pavilions of the Ospedale Civile has been named after him: on its facade, facing the internal garden, a plaque with a bronze effigy commemorates him. On the roof of the same building is also the helicopter landing pad for the emergency service (the only one in Venice), which bears the name 'JONA'.
Another plaque in his memory is placed in the Venice Ghetto, on the facade of the Jewish Rest Home.
Still in the Cannaregio district, on Strada Nova at number 3826, a *Stolperstein* (stumbling block) was laid in 2020 in memory of his sacrifice, bearing the inscription: 'Here lived Giuseppe Jona – Born 1888 – Sought refuge in death – 17.09.1943'.

The world's most intrepid parachutist

In the Catholic cemetery of San Nicolò, to the right of the small chapel-oratory dedicated to St Joseph, right at the end of the path leading to its entrance, stands a cypress tree.

It was at the foot of this tree that on 3 May 1953, around 6.30pm, the final flight of Salvatore Cannarozzo ended. He was an extraordinary parachutist of international renown whom the French loved to call '*le parachutiste le plus intrépide du monde*' ('the world's most intrepid parachutist').

Cannarozzo jumped from a height of 3,000 metres and had planned an extremely low-altitude opening. This highly demanding manoeuvre was one he had mastered as one of the world's leading experts.

Unfortunately, something in the parachute's opening mechanism failed and there was no escape for the Sicilian athlete.

Some witnesses reported a final, desperate cry; others recounted the parachutist struck one of the cypress trees before hitting the ground; still others claimed he bounced off the cemetery chapel.

The impact with the ground was so forceful that it created a compression in the earth, almost a hollow, which remained visible for many years.
Salvatore Cannarozzo was born in Balestrate (Palermo, Sicily) on 5 April 1921 and was considered a hero in the world of parachuting: he was among the first to practise manual deployment, also achieving the world record for low-altitude opening.
He won the first World Championship in precision landing from 600 metres and also tested the fabric wings designed by Léo Valentin.
He was the first Italian parachutist to jump from a helicopter.
For many years there was a vase of flowers at the site of the tragedy, but it has long since disappeared.
There is hope that a plaque will be placed at the foot of that cypress tree, to commemorate that tragic event and to honour the memory of Salvatore Cannarozzo. A group of aviation enthusiasts are already working to make this tribute a reality.

BRICKS ON THE SAND

7

The remains of the St Mark's bell tower that collapsed in 1902

San Nicolò Beach – Lido di Venice
Accessible by bus from Santa Maria Elisabetta Passenger Terminal: line A

t's strange to walk along the beach and see fragments of bricks of various sizes, sometimes even whole ones, scattered on the sand with apparent logic.

These aren't illegally dumped building waste, but bricks deposited the shore by the sea.

On the morning of 14 July 1902, the bell tower of St Mark's, known cally as '*el paron de casa*' ('the master of the house'), collapsed in on self. The event came as no surprise: the precarious stability of the bell wer had been known for some time.

At 9.47am on that summer Monday, the bell tower came down probably the least destructive way possible, sparing the basilica d causing relatively minor damage compared with what could have appened had the dynamics of the fall been different. Fortunately, ere were no fatalities. That very evening, the then mayor of Venice, lippo Grimani, uttered his famous phrase regarding its reconstruction: *ov'era e com'era*' ('Where it was and as it was').

The work of removing and salvaging material was entrusted to the chitect Giacomo Boni, who saved what he could of the stone and ronze decorations so they could be reinstalled in the new building. nce the debris was cleared, the tower's foundations were exposed, vealing even more ancient finds, including Byzantine decorations and Hellenistic stone head.

Two weeks after the collapse, architect Boni planned to dump the usable parts at sea. It was decided to take them out of the Lido, about ree miles from the coast, so as not to interfere with navigation in any ay.

For the first of the numerous trips carrying the rubble out to sea, a remony was organised.

On the barge where the material had been loaded, a brick was placed, rapped in laurel, inscribed with the date 14 July 1902.

A procession set off from St Mark's heading towards the open sea, here Gigetta Alessandri (daughter of the painter Angelo Alessandri), osen as the young sponsor of the ceremony, threw the brick to mark e start of the sinking of the bricks.

Over the years, storms and currents have caused many of these bricks be pushed towards San Nicolò beach, where they've been appearing the shore for several decades.

LIDO DI VENEZIA PLANETARIUM

A very interesting place, only open on Sunday afternoons

Parco pubblico Askenasi (former Luna Park)
Lungomare D'Annunzio, Lido di Venice
astrovenezia.net
Open for schools and groups by appointment and on Sunday afternoons (October–May)
Accessible by bus from Santa Maria Elisabetta Passenger Terminal: line A

On Lungomare D'Annunzio there once stood the beautiful Luna Park, built between 1931 and 1932 to designs by the Milanese chitect Antonio Cassi Ramelli. It was largely dismantled before the cond World War. Today the site is occupied by Parco Askenasi, though me of the old amusement park's brick structures have survived, such the entrance pavilions and the building that housed the little theatre.

The former theatre building has been home since 2003 to the enetian Amateur Astronomers Association. In 1983, the association ecided to build a planetarium for Venice. It was inaugurated in 1986 at e association's first home in the former convent of San Nicolò, before oving to its current location.

Being somewhat off the beaten track and only open on Sunday ternoons, the planetarium is unknown to most people.

Inside, a projector equipped with a complex optical system mprising motors and 1,800 lenses, specially crafted by Ottiche Zen, n reproduce various astronomical situations and circumstances on a emispherical dome 8.2 metres in diameter, which serves as a screen.

The planetarium offers a fascinating variety of scenarios: from the y as it would appear from a boat in the middle of St Mark's Basin to hat would be observed from the North Pole or the equator. You can so observe astronomical conditions as our ancestors would have seen em or as they will appear in the future.

There's also a simulation, through a very evocative video projection, f what would happen to Venice if northern Italy were struck by a eteorite.

What makes this planetarium special is that, unlike today's digital anetariums that use fisheye projectors, this is a genuine marvel of pure echanics.

The main hall, with its 60 seats, hosts conferences, in-depth meetings d lessons for schools or interested groups.

Inside you can admire several meteorites, as well as telescopes and her instruments for astronomical observation.

The building also houses seismographs, some belonging to the ational Institute of Geophysics and Volcanology, and a station for bserving meteors using radio systems.

FALCONI NAVAL WORKSHOP MUSEUM

A dream destination for sea enthusiasts

Via Biagio Zulian, 11
Lido di Venezia
Visits by appointment only: 0348 450 3766
Free admission
10-minute walk from Santa Maria Elisabetta Passenger Terminal

Hidden among the houses on a quiet street in the Lido, the Falconi Naval Workshop Museum is exactly what no one would expect to nd here. In the outdoor section of the complex, amid an incredible ariety of objects, you can see propellers, rudders, chains, lifeboats, an nsaldo engine that belonged to the training ship Marinaretto, and even working submarine capable of carrying three operators and diving to depth of 500 metres.

Inside stands a large wooden statue representing Justice, created r the project to reconstruct the new Bucintoro, the famous doge's eremonial barge destroyed in 1797. Unfortunately, for various asons – mainly financial – this evocative and fascinating initiative has ot yet come to fruition.

The museum houses thousands of nautical objects: compasses, xtants, bells, echo sounders, diving suits, nautical charts, knots, aques, numerous maritime paintings by the artist Giacomo Vaccaro, ooks and other items collected from around the world over several ecades.

This authentic dream destination for sea lovers was created by ommander Ferruccio Falconi, former Chief Pilot of the Port of Venice, man with a truly remarkable biography and a genuine icon of Italian afaring. His sons have also contributed to bringing this unique place life. Andrea, an expert deep-sea diver, formerly a petty officer in the alian Navy, and Nicola, formerly a petty officer with the Lagunari, ave both made significant contributions to maritime research.

Their published works are rich and fascinating, drawing on decades experience at sea. They've written about the discovery of the steamship larianna and various wrecks in the Gulf of Venice, among other ndings from their survey of over 150 kilometres of Veneto coastline.

Entering the Falconi Workshop Museum is an incredible experience; ou can feel the passion and love these three people have for the sea, to hich they've dedicated their lives.

It's a total immersion in the world of navigation and its technical olution – a continuous discovery, one surprise after another!

MAIALIDO MUSEUM

A museum in a dental surgery waiting room

Via Sandro Gallo 80/C
Lido di Venice
Visits by appointment only
renzo@maialido.it
maialido.it
Free admission
Accessible by bus from Santa Maria Elisabetta Passenger Terminal: lines A–B–C

The world is full of strange and original museums, but the Lido of Venice is home to something particularly unusual. Not far from the Ponte delle Quattro Fontane, on the ground floor of a villa facing the main road, you'll find a museum in the waiting rooms of a working dental surgery.

The Maialido Museum is the world's second-largest collection of objects dedicated to a single animal: the pig.

Here you can find it represented in over 30,000 objects including postcards, paintings, prints, statues and figurines made from the most diverse materials, from glass to ceramics, terracotta to plastic, steel to bronze, silver to gold.

This extraordinary collection was assembled by Dr Renzo Battaglia, a dentist.

Born in 1949, he lives in Padua but has practised on the Lido of Venice for over 40 years, visiting twice a week.

His interest in collecting pig-related objects began almost by chance in 1976, when a friend gave him a little Murano glass pig.

From there began a genuine passion that led him to buy – but above all to receive as gifts – objects depicting the pig in all its symbolic forms, from the most profound to the most ironic.

Among the thousands of objects, both handcrafted and mass-produced, there are also authentic works of art by Nespoli, Cuoghi, Musante and Potenza.

Dr Battaglia has held numerous exhibitions showcasing selected pieces from his vast collection. After all, the pig is a fascinating animal, rich in symbolism and used as a metaphor by many artists, including the writer George Orwell in *Animal Farm* and by Pink Floyd in their album *Animals*.

The Maialido Museum can be visited free of charge by appointment and is generally always open during the Venice International Film Festival, whose main venue is only a few hundred metres away.

Only Stockholm's Pig Museum has a larger collection.

Above the entrance door hangs a charming statue of a pig.

PROJECTION HOLES AT THE HOTEL EXCELSIOR

(11)

It was through these two secret openings that projectionists screened the films of the first film festival in 1932

Lungomare Guglielmo Marconi, 41
Lido di Venezia
Accessible during the hotel's opening months (April–October) and by bus from Santa Maria Elisabetta Passenger Terminal: line V

On 6 August 1932, cinema officially entered the world of art! The setting for this extraordinary event was neither Paris nor Hollywood, but the Lido of Venice.

It was here, as part of the 18th Venice Biennale, that the first International Exhibition of Cinematographic Art took place at the Hotel Excelsior from 6 to 21 August.

What remains, nearly a century later, of that first film festival in the world?

The Hotel Excelsior has undergone restoration and modifications over time, but two holes still remain as testament to that historic event. They sit above the door that today leads to the swimming pool, while back then it led to the garden where the screenings took place.

Almost no one notices these holes of enormous historical importance. Through these two openings, projectionists screened 40 films from six different nations in their original languages for the audience. It was a cultural and social event attended by famous figures and distinguished guests, including Prince Umberto of Savoy and his consort, the Prince of Wales, Winston Churchill, Henry Ford and actors of the calibre of Greta Garbo and Clark Gable, to name just a few.

The festival opened with the screening of the film *Dr. Jekyll and Mr. Hyde*. Except for this first screening held inside to avoid interruptions due to bad weather, screenings at the festival always took place outdoors.

The person who conceived and championed all this, with the intention of relaunching the Lido on the international stage, was the then Minister of Finance and President of the Biennale, Giuseppe Volpi, Count of Misurata, a man of brilliant and visionary insight.

In 1937, the International Exhibition of Cinematographic Art was moved to the nearby Palazzo del Cinema, built that same year to a design by engineer Qualiata.

The Hotel Excelsior, however, continues to be a focal point for this important event: over the years it has hosted almost all of the actors and directors who have shaped the history of cinema.

COAT OF ARMS OF THE ALBERTI FAMILY

12

The house of the first Italian-American in history

Relais Alberti
Campo della Chiesa
Malamocco-Lido di Venice
relaisalberti.com
Accessible by bus from Santa Maria Elisabetta Passenger Terminal: lines A-B

Overlooking Campo della Chiesa in Malamocco, the Relais Alberti is an elegant hotel housed in a 16th-century palazzo that has survived various upheavals over centuries. Above the fireplace in the main salon you can see the ancient coat of arms of the Alberti family. The relais takes its name from the noble family of Florentine origin who once owned it. This was home to the man considered the first Italian–American in history.

Known to everyone as Pietro (probably in memory of a brother who died in infancy), Giulio Cesare Alberti was born on 2 June 1608 to Andrea Alberti, secretary of the ducal treasury, and his wife Veronica.

The exact reasons that prompted him to leave Malamocco for the Dutch colony of New Amsterdam (present-day New York), are unknown. What is certain is that during Pietro Cesare Alberti's youth, relations between Venetians and the Dutch were good, as they were allies during the Thirty Years' War, and over three hundred soldiers from the Netherlands were garrisoned in Venice. Between 1630 and 1632, these troops moved to Malamocco to escape the plague.

According to chronicles, Pietro Cesare Alberti converted to the Protestant faith and became a sailor in the service of Commander David Pietersen de Vries and landed in New Amsterdam on 2 June 1635.

Colonial records refer to him by various names, such as Peter Ceser, Pieter Cesar, Peter Cesar Alberto, sometimes accompanied by the nickname Mallemock (referring to Malamocco).

Business must have gone well for him, as a few years later he bought an estate in present-day Brooklyn and, eight years after that, another property in present-day Manhattan.

Being the first Italian to settle permanently in the 'New World', Pietro Cesare Alberti is considered the first Italian–American in history.

He and his wife died on 9 November 1655, probably after an Indian attack, leaving six children orphaned (another had died in infancy).

Their descendants now bear the surnames Burtis and Alburtis.

The palazzo, along with the neighbouring Ca' del Borgo, long belonged to the Canossian sisters, who taught countless girls from Malamocco to sew and embroider here.

MIRACULOUS CHRIST OF POVEGLIA

13

A crucifix miraculously recovered from the sea in the early 1300s

Parish Church of Santa Maria Assunta
Campo della Chiesa, 1
Malamocco – Lido di Venice
Sunday and public holidays 9am–10am (Mass time)
Accessible by bus from the Santa Maria Elisabetta Passenger Terminal: lines A and B

Since 1809, the Parish Church of Santa Maria Assunta in Malamocco has housed several precious works originally from the ow-demolished church of San Vitale in Poveglia. Among these is the mous miraculous crucifix, distinguished by its unique features: the ead is covered with reddish-brown hair and encircled by a crown of orns made from braided rope, reminiscent of ship rigging.

It is considered miraculous because it was reportedly recovered from e sea by Poveglia fishermen in the early 14th century.

After a restoration in 1983, some studies attributed it to a 14th-ntury Venetian sculptor, emphasising the originality of its materials. thers, noting its similarity to crucifixes in Piran and Split (modern-ay Croatia), suggest it belongs to the Dalmatian school.

Veneration of this work is very old: sailors would turn to it during orms, and each time a ship was miraculously saved, offerings – cluding weapons – were brought to the church of San Vitale.

The devotion was so strong that even after Poveglia was largely andoned, the church remained well cared for. Ships passing through e Poveglia canal would traditionally salute the Christ with a cannon olley.

The feast of the Crucifix of Poveglia is still celebrated annually on 14 eptember in the church of Santa Maria Assunta.

Another piece brought from the church of San Vitale is the painting *Virgin in Prayer* (1736) by Giulia Lama (1681–1747), one of her most elaborate works.

Giulia was probably the first female painter in Venice to receive church commissions and one of the first to practise nude drawing. Although known in her time, she was only recently rediscovered. Unlike Rosalba Carriera, who travelled widely across Europe, Giulia Lama was born and died in Venice, never married, and her art was never recognised as a profession during her lifetime.

The painting underwent major restoration in 2023–2024, which restored it to its original splendour.

LIONS OF MALAMOCCO

The only place in the lagoon where the lions of the Venetian Republic still survive, despite the leontoclasia of 1797

Campo della Chiesa, Piazza Maggiore, Palazzo del Podestà, Rio de le Munegh and other locations
Malamocco – Lido di Venice
Accessible by bus from the Santa Maria Elisabetta Passenger Terminal: lines A B, and C

When the glorious era of the Serenissima Republic ended in 1797, hundreds of carved lions – symbols of St Mark – could be found ross Venice and the lagoon islands, on wellheads, palaces, bridges and ore.

By 25 May of that year, the Venetian Committee of Public Safety, ıder orders from Napoleon Bonaparte, decreed that all lions considered nblems of the former government should be removed.

This led to a remarkable – and highly improbable – attempt at *ımnatio memoriae*, carried out by a Venetian stonecutter from San ːonardo named Beneto Giraldon. For 1,980 silver ducats, he provided list of lions and lion mouths to be secretly reported and destroyed.

The exact number of lions removed with chisels is unknown, but was certainly significant. Some survived, but large-scale losses of onework were recorded almost everywhere. Traces of these lions can ill be seen in many places, particularly on the panels of empty and arred wellheads.

Some images are preserved in contemporary paintings, offering a impse of what squares, palaces, and other sites looked like before this ːstructive campaign. Remarkably, Malamocco appears to have been ared. This event has been termed *leontoclasia*, borrowing the Greek *'astos*, meaning 'to break', similar to the term *iconoclasia* used for ligious iconoclasm.

The ancient Lido village can proudly claim to be the only place in ıe lagoon where all the lions that witnessed the fall of the Republic are ill found.

Two lions remain in the Palazzo del Podestà, one facing the lagoon ıd one toward the church square; another three can be seen on the des of the three main wellheads; and one is carved on the flagpole ıse in front of the church of Santa Maria Assunta. One more lion ands nearby, at the lagoon boundary marker of 1791 on the Rio de le luneghete. Additional lions can also be found on the facades of various ːivate homes.

There is no definitive evidence as to why the lions of Malamocco ere spared, but oral tradition relates that the inhabitants took a ːcidedly hostile stance toward Giraldon's stonecutters. The stonecutters seeing the village's isolated position but above all wishing to preserve ıeir own safety – decided to postpone the work and never returned to lalamocco.

TRACES OF FORTE ALBERONI

The forgotten military fort

Circolo Golf Venezia
Strada Vecchia dei Bagni, 1, Alberoni – Lido di Venice
041 731333 – info@circologolfvenezia.it
Tuesday to Sunday: 8.30am–6pm
Golf course visits by appointment: contact the secretary
Accessible by bus from the Santa Maria Elisabetta Passenger Terminal: line A
Club house open to the public

Just a stone's throw from the beach and the sea of the Lido, in the Alberoni area, the Circolo Golf Venezia is hardly a secret in the goon. Yet few know that this area was once home to Forte Alberoni, ilt by the Serenissima between 1646 and 1650.

To reach the golf course, visitors cross a footbridge spanning a small ock (part of the canal that once surrounded the fort) and pass a bastion arked with the words 'Golf Club Venezia'. A few metres further on, e austere silhouette of a historic brick and marble building appears, its riginal military purpose unmistakable.

Just a short distance from the clubhouse stands the casemate of Forte lberoni, a key military installation that, together with Forte San Pietro ocated opposite, beyond the Malamocco port entrance), completed e Venetian defensive system devised during the 16th century.

In the 19th century, both the French and the Austrians made odifications and reinforcements to the fort, which remained in use en during World War I.

The idea to transform the site reportedly came from Henry Ford, the famous American automobile magnate. In 1926, during a stay at the Hotel Excelsior, he expressed to Count Giuseppe Volpi his desire to play golf. At the time, no Lido facility could accommodate him, but Count Volpi took action. In 1928, the area – no longer used for military purposes – was leased to CIGA (Compagnia Italiana Grandi Alberghi). A nine-hole course opened in 1930 and expanded to 18 holes by 1951. The course design benefited from the expertise of Scottish golfer Bobby Cruickshank and was built by the Glasgow firm Maxwell M. Hart.

A meeting between Mussolini and Hitler

In 1934, Benito Mussolini and Adolf Hitler met here during Hitler's first official trip abroad as head of state.

The lunch took place in the space now occupied by the clubhouse. The two leaders were reportedly seen talking at length near the well, which still stands on the practice course today.

PILOTS' TOWER

An important vantage point

Strada della Droma, 126
Alberoni, Lido di Venice
Visits by request for educational purposes: amministrazione@pilotivenezia.it
Accessible by bus from the Santa Maria Elisabetta Passenger Terminal: line A

The Pilots' Tower immediately catches the eye: a concrete column supports an octagonal platform more than 30 metres above the round, offering a 360-degree view. By day, it unmistakably appears as a ookout. By night or in foggy conditions, it can imaginatively resemble flying saucer.

The tower serves as a viewpoint and coordination centre for maritime affic entering and leaving the lagoon.

Since 1 January 1973, it has monitored every movement within the goon and in the roadstead off the Lido of Venice using a network of adars. Here, ships at anchor await their turn to enter the commercial ort of Marghera.

From the tower, pilots of the Port of Venice set off and return aboard ecialised boats known as *pilotine*, guiding vessels along the Canale dei etroli and the channels of Porto Marghera.

Boarding and disembarking these vessels is a spectacular sight: pilots ap literally in mid-air from the pilotina to a moving ship, or vice versa, ith impressive precision.

At the foot of the tower stands a building that functions as a small museum, housing numerous items recovered from ships and other boats. In the adjacent garden or leaning against the structure, visitors can see old anchors, propellers, a large rudder and various marble bas-reliefs.

Since the Pilots' Tower is operational 365 days a year, visits are rare and strictly educational, and must be arranged in advance.

CANNONS OF THE OUTER ALBERONI BREAKWATER

17

Old English cannons repurposed as mooring posts

Accessible all year, on foot only

Anyone walking along the Alberoni breakwater will likely notice a series of unusual protrusions along the path.

Strangely, these are old muzzle-loading cannons, rendered harmless nd used in the construction of the 19th-century breakwaters at the ntrance to the lagoon as mooring posts for Austro–Venetian naval essels.

It's a curious example of reuse: decommissioned guns from various efensive batteries were converted for engineering purposes. The reeches of the cannons, embedded in the breakwater and set in ozzolana cement, jut out at regular intervals along the walkway.

Research was conducted on six cannons removed from the reakwaters during the construction of MOSE, the engineering project esigned to protect Venice and the Venetian Lagoon from high tides nd flooding. Five of the cannons came from Santa Maria del Mare, and ne from Alberoni. The investigation revealed that all six were made in ngland – five in the mid-18th century and one in the 19th century. ach cannon weighs around 2.9 tonnes.

Numerous anchors of various types were also embedded in the reakwater for mooring purposes. Some were recovered during the nstallation of the movable barriers designed to protect Venice from igh water.

Today, the cannons and anchors that have been brought to the urface are awaiting placement in a museum or an old fort, with several leas and proposals under consideration.

Along the Alberoni breakwater, a number of cannons remain in situ. While no longer used for mooring, they bear witness to a centuries-old istory lived on the edge of the sea.

TRACES OF LANDFALL 18

Where the sea meets art

Alberoni breakwater
Accessible by bus from the Santa Maria Elisabetta Passenger Terminal: line A

On one of the poles supporting the cable that carries electricity to the lighthouse at the end of the breakwater, a large metal 'cabinet' bears a painted eye and the word 'OCIO' in Venetian dialect, meaning 'Watch out! Be careful!'

Faded though they now are, a few paintings can still be seen on the concrete blocks lining the tip of the Alberoni breakwater, around the building that houses the lighthouse. These are the last remnants of what was once, in the early 2000s, a remarkable international art event conceived by the eclectic and energetic architect Antonio Rodriguez (1948–2011).

Born in Brescia to an Italian mother and a Spanish father, Rodriguez spent most of his life in Switzerland's Ticino canton. He was not only an architect and builder but also a versatile artist, working as a poet, painter and sculptor. Known for his warmth, charm and slightly eccentric appearance, he was rarely seen without his dog, Area.

Rodriguez arrived at the Lido by chance and immediately fell in love with the Alberoni area. He spent many of his summers there and visited every two weeks, bringing a wave of art and culture to the area. He organised exhibitions, performances and ecological initiatives, such as clearing the beach after winter storms. Every year, on the first weekend of July, he staged an artistic event at the tip of the breakwater known as the Landfall Art Center.

The event drew artists from across Italy, as well as from France, Switzerland and even South America. All works were created on-site using only materials recovered from the breakwater or the beach. Originally intended as an ecological awareness project, it soon became a high-level creative laboratory, attracting media attention year after year.

The 2005 edition was particularly notable, dedicated to Hugo Pratt, the artist who owned a house in the old village of Malamocco.

The construction works for MOSE, the engineering project designed to protect Venice and the Venetian Lagoon from high tides and flooding, brought the event to a halt, and the subsequent passing of Antonio Rodriguez marked its definitive end.

Today, memories, photographs and traces on the breakwater are all that remain of this unique initiative that shaped summers at Alberoni for several years.

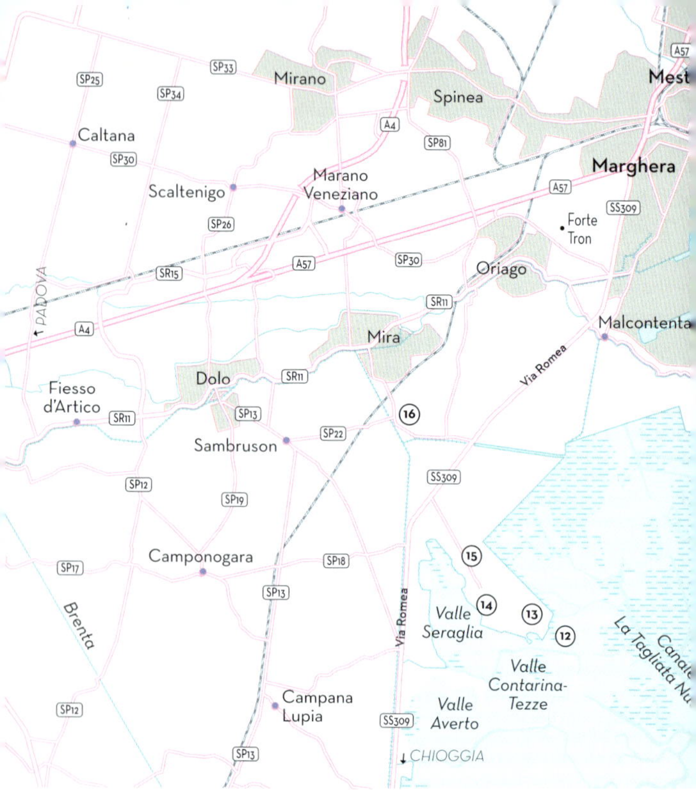

Central Lagoon

SR14
SS14
Aeroporto
Marco Polo di Venezia
Torcello
Campalto
Palude
del Monte
Burano
Parco
San Giuliano
Treporti
Campalto
Murano
Ponte della Libertà
Sant'Erasmo
SP14
Canale di Treporti
Ca'Savio
San Michele
Le Vignole
Venezia
La Certosa
Faro Pagoda
Boca
di Porto
di Lido
1
2
Lido
San Clemente
5
3
6
4
Sacca Sessola
7
Canale delle Scoazze
Santo Spirito
Isola
di Lido
8
Poveglia
9
Mare
Adriatico
Malamocco
N
10
Alberoni
Spignon
11
0
5
10 km

1

MUSEUM OF MADNESS, SAN SERVOLO

The former Central Asylum of Veneto

San Servolo Island
041 8627167 (Monday–Friday, 9am–1pm)
Thursday 2pm–5.30pm, Friday to Sunday 9.45am–4.30pm
Accessible by ACTV motorboat line 20 from the San Zaccaria pier (Piazza San Marco)

The island of San Servolo, which today houses a conference centre and the Venice International University, has been home to the Museum of the Asylum since 2006. From 1725, the island served as a facility for noble patients with mental disorders. During the Napoleonic era, the asylum opened to all people with psychiatric conditions, regardless of social class.

From 1804, the hospital became the central asylum for all the Venetian provinces, Dalmatia, and Tyrol. In 1932, it was formally designated a psychiatric hospital, a status it retained until 1978, when such institutions were closed under the Basaglia Law.

The museum displays numerous records and objects documenting the care and confinement of patients. It also highlights early forms of music therapy and occupational therapy, which were advanced practices at San Servolo compared with other institutions of the time.

Visitors to the museum can also enter the historic pharmacy, a fascinating room containing 256 pharmaceutical jars donated by the Venetian Republic in the first half of the 18th century, each marked with the lion's emblem. Many of the herbs used were grown directly on the island.

The pharmacy also used so-called healing stones, including garnets, oriental hyacinths, corals, mother of pearl and bezoar stones. The latter is a concretion of hair and plant fibres formed in the digestive tract of ruminants, and was believed to neutralise poisons.

On a central work table, visitors can see pages from an 18th-century pharmacopoeia listing medicinal herbs and recipes. In 1809, the pharmacy became the General Pharmacy. While continuing to serve the hospital, it also prepared medicines for the poor associated with the 30 confraternities of Venice.

The history of San Servolo begins with a Benedictine monastic settlement in the 7th century, followed by the arrival of Benedictine nuns from the convent of Saints Leone and Basso in Malamocco. Later, nuns from other orders, arriving from Candia (modern Crete), settled on the island. Around 1715, the island became a military hospital and was entrusted to the Order of Hospitaller Fathers of Saint John of God, who built the present church designed by Tommaso Temanza. Only later was an asylum opened for noble patients with mental disorders (see above).

MUMMY OF NEMENKHET-AMON

2

The most important Egyptian artefact in the lagoon

Museum of San Lazzaro degli Armeni
Island of San Lazzaro degli Armeni
041 5260104
Visits by appointment only
visite@mechitar.org
Vaporetto: line 20

Among the many works and artefacts in the Armenian monastery's remarkable collection on San Lazzaro, one stands out unexpectedly and captures the attention of every visitor: the mummy of the vizier Nemenkhet-Amon.

It was through the study of the wooden sarcophagus that contained him, and particularly the hieroglyphic inscriptions on one of its sides, that scholars were able to identify the mummy.

Documents show that the sarcophagus arrived on the island on 18 July 1825, donated by the Egyptian Foreign Minister, Boghos Bey Yusufian.

Experts consider the mummy a 'superb example of bandaging'. In 1995, it underwent radiocarbon dating, which revised previous estimates and placed it between the end of the Third Intermediate Period and the start of the Twenty-Sixth Dynasty, in the 7th and 6th centuries BCE.

Also dating from this period is the decorative net covering the mummy, made of multicoloured beads featuring geometric diamond patterns and symbolic images of deities associated with the Egyptian afterlife.

Lord Byron on San Lazzaro degli Armeni

Lord Byron arrived in Venice in 1816 to escape scandal. During his time in the lagoon city, he enjoyed a period of freedom and indulgence, documented in his letters, which describe his relationships and active social life.

Byron was also an enthusiastic swimmer. He loved swimming in the canals and the lagoon, inspiring a local fashion and the creation of the Byron Cup, a swimming race between the Lido di Venezia and the railway station, held until 1949.

Venice had a profound impact on the English poet's literary work, with its unique atmosphere and Oriental charm. During his stay, he also studied Armenian at the San Lazzaro monastery. This period was crucial for Byron, marking a break with his past and the start of his unconventional lifestyle.

CIRCULAR LIBRARY OF SAN LAZZARO DEGLI ARMENI

③

The largest collection of Armenian manuscripts in the West

Island of San Lazzaro degli Armeni
041 5260104
Visits by appointment only
visite@mechitar.org
Vaporetto: line 20

Designed by architect Andon Ispenian in 1977, a circular building on San Lazzaro degli Armeni houses one of the island's greatest treasures: a library containing the largest collection of Armenian manuscripts in the Western world.

Among the collection, notable works include texts on archaeology donated by the Egyptian minister Artin Cerakian in the early 20th century, the *Tetravangelo of Queen Mlk, and the Romance of Alexander*, which tells the life of Alexander the Great and is believed by some to have been produced in Cilicia, in southern Turkey.

A curious feature is that if you stand in the centre of the library, directly above the circle marked on the floor, and speak, your voice is curiously amplified. This effect is due to the semicircular ceiling, which carries sound throughout the space.

Alphabets and printing in the lagoon

For more than two centuries, San Lazzaro degli Armeni was home to a renowned printing press. Visitors to the island can still see the machinery that was used here.

The press is closely linked to the work of Abbot Mechitar, who arrived in Venice in 1715 to establish a religious community dedicated to spreading European culture in Armenia and Armenian culture in Europe. Venice was the ideal location, offering freedom to print and trade.

Initially, Mechitar collaborated with the press of Antonio Bortoli. At the time, he was the only printer with the sought-after Armenian typefaces. For many years, books were composed on San Lazzaro, with the type being transported by boat to the press and then returned to the island.

In 1729, thanks to an anonymous benefactor, the Abbot was able to buy the typefaces and presses from an abandoned printing workshop owned by Vardapet Oskan, who had moved to Amsterdam. The equipment arrived on the island in 1789, and the press flourished until its closure in 1995.

RELIEF OF THE PLAGUE SAINTS

4

The world's first site dedicated to isolating people with contagious diseases

Isola del Lazzaretto Vecchio
info@lazzarettiveneziani.it
Visible from the outside, either from the shores of the Lido or by boat
Currently under restoration (visits soon possible)

In 1423, a decree from the Venetian Senate established, for the first time anywhere, a hospital on the island of Lazzaretto Vecchio dedicated to caring for and isolating those suffering from the plague.

At that time, the island was dedicated to Saint Mary of Nazareth and was initially named Nazaretum before later becoming known as Lazzaretto

This name was a clear reference to Saint Lazarus the Beggar, a poor man covered in sores who appears in a parable in the Gospel of Luke (16:19–31) lying at the rich man's door, hoping for crumbs from his table. He became the patron saint of lepers and the poor in general, as well as of the sick and suffering, and was invoked as a protector against the plague and all contagious diseases.

At the Tèzon Vecchio, above a handsome marble portal from the 16th century, an inscription recalls the building's construction, ordered by the Procurators of Saint Mark de Citra in the month of May 1565.' On either side of the figure of Saint Mark are two other saints associated with the plague: Saint Sebastian and Saint Roch, alongside Saint Lazarus.

The arrows that pierced Saint Sebastian were seen as symbols of wounds, particularly those caused by the bubonic plague, which was regarded as divine punishment.

Sebastian's survival was interpreted as a sign of heavenly protection, and he became a much venerated figure during epidemics, with the faithful praying for his intercession to protect them from illness.

His cult was closely associated with that of Saint Roch, whom Venice regarded as a model of good behaviour; after contracting the plague, Saint Roch retreated to the woods to avoid spreading the infection. During his isolation, a dog cared for him, bringing him food each day and helping him recover.

Miraculously cured, Roch continued to care for plague victims, travelling and tending to the sick in every town and village he passed through.

On returning to his homeland, he was unjustly imprisoned and died in jail.

Venice, with its dense trading networks and constant international contacts, was especially vulnerable to epidemics. Invoking the saints was a central part of the city's public response to such crises.

Adopting Saint Sebastian and Saint Roch as protectors reflected Christian tradition and was a spiritual strategy to face the waves of plague that struck the city.

The veneration of these saints became a central aspect of Venice's religious and cultural life, inspiring churches, confraternities and works of art dedicated to their memory and intercession.

The other plague island

In 1468, to further prevent the spread of plague, the Venetian Senate ordered the construction of another lazzaretto, still known today as the Lazzaretto Nuovo (see p. 104).

MOROSINI FUNERARY MONUMENTS

5

A family that made the church their mausoleum

Church of San Clemente
San Clemente Island
First Tuesday of every month: 9.30am–12.30pm
Reachable via the hotel's private shuttle (free), departing every 30 minutes from the San Marco dock

On the left-hand side of the Church of San Clemente, just before the majestic replica of the House of Loreto (see following double page), is a commemorative plaque. Flanking it are two telamons supporting a frieze decorated with arms and armour. Above, a statue depicts a commander between two angels holding his helmet and general's hat. This is the funerary monument of Giorgio Morosini, who died in 1676.

Opposite stands the memorial dedicated to Giorgio's younger brothers, Pietro and Lorenzo Morosini, who died in 1683 and 1686 respectively. The funerary monuments, intended to house the Morosini family remains, were commissioned from the Flemish artist Juste Le Court by Pietro and Lorenzo themselves. The upper part once featured busts of the two brothers, now missing, surmounted by a striking figure of Justice that survives today. Many of the statues and other elements of the monument were removed in 1992. Some were recovered in 2002 and placed in the Museum of Sacred Art at Sant'Apollonia, which is now closed.

Of the buildings comprising the San Clemente complex, the church is the oldest. The first records date back to 1131–1134, when the wealthy merchant Pietro Gattilesso founded a hospital with an adjoining church dedicated to Saint Clement. The complex was managed by the Canons Regular of Saint Augustine, and in 1288 the relics of Saint Anianus of Alexandria, a disciple of Saint Mark the Evangelist, were transferred here.

In 1432, Pope Eugene IV Condulmer installed the Monks of Charity, who oversaw a significant phase of renovations affecting the church and the convent. The island was a frequent stop for Venetian patricians, particularly for medical reasons during the recurrent plague epidemics. Wealthy benefactors often made generous donations to the convent to embellish the church, and these funds were frequently used to create private chapels. In 1645 the island passed into the hands of the Camaldolese Hermits of Monte Corona. In 1652, the Morosini family funded the work on the church facade, dedicating it to the deeds of Francesco and Tommaso Morosini, who had died in the Cretan War. Sculptor Andrea Cominelli created statues of Saint Benedict and Saint Romuald in the two upper niches, while the lateral parts of the facade feature epigraphs with bas-reliefs depicting battles in which the Morosini had fought. The original Madonna and Child was moved to the upper section of the church, and above the door Cominelli placed the Morosini coat of arms, cementing the family's near-exclusive association with the church as their mausoleum.

Over time, the church became a treasure trove. Many of its riches were lost, except for one of particular value: the wooden sacristy, which was recovered and placed in the Church of Ognissanti in Venice.

THE HOUSE OF LORETO INSIDE THE CHURCH OF SAN CLEMENTE

6

A replica of the house where the Virgin Mary lived in Nazareth

San Clemente Island
Accessible by the hotel's private shuttle service (free), departing every 30 minutes from the San Marco pier

The church on San Clemente Island holds a genuine curiosity: by order of the Patriarchal Vicar Monsignor Francesco Lazzaroni, a eplica of the House of Loreto – the house where the Virgin Mary lived ı Nazareth – was built inside the church in the 17th century, much like he one in the Church of San Pantalon in Venice (see the guide *Secret 'enice* from the same publisher).

During the plague of 1630, Lazzaroni vowed to make a pilgrimage o the Sanctuary of Loreto (in the province of Ancona, in the Marche egion), but ill health prevented him from keeping his promise. Instead, e fulfilled his vow by commissioning a replica of the holy house. Jnable to build it in the Church of Sant'Angelo, where he was parish riest, he chose the church on this island, which was in need of major estoration.

In 1646, a polychrome cedarwood statue of the Black Madonna and Child was installed inside, quickly becoming an object of great devotion. 'oday, this statue can be seen in the Church of Ognissanti, Venice.

The church was enlarged in 1662, and the replica of the House of oreto was dismantled, then reassembled and enriched with bas-reliefs epicting scenes from the life of the Virgin.

In 1703, a beautiful black stone bas-relief by the Bolognese artist Giuseppe Maria Mazza was added, showing the Nativity and the doration of the Shepherds.

The interior of the holy house mirrors the original in the Marche: imple exposed brickwork, fragments of wall paintings and a ceiling ainted blue with golden stars.

Unfortunately, mainly due to damp, the condition of the wall aintings is very poor.

After the fall of the Venetian Republic, the Camaldolese monks emained on the island until 1810. The site then changed use several imes, serving first as a military acility, and later as a psychiatric ospital. Most of the church's lecoration was dispersed, though ome works are safeguarded lsewhere or held in storage by he heritage authorities. Today, he church is largely empty, apart rom a few stone memorials, some aintings and a striking crucifix.

San Clemente and Manzoni's plague

It was July 1630 when the Marquis of Strigis, ambassador to the Duke of Mantua, arrived on the island of San Clemente for a diplomatic visit, with his entourage. He showed clear symptoms of illness upon arrival. Yet, despite growing concerns over his health, the Republic of Venice – out of respect for his high status – chose not to confine him to the Lazzaretto (the quarantine island), and instead allowed him to remain on San Clemente. It wasn't long before the disease took hold: the marquis and five of his servants soon passed away from the illness.

At the time, maintenance works were under way on the island. Among the workers was Giovanni Maria Tirinello, a carpenter from Venice who lived near Campo Sant'Agnese. He contracted the disease and, unknowingly, carried it back to the city, where it spread rapidly.

The seriousness of the outbreak was immediately apparent. On 15 August of that year, huge numbers of Venetians – particularly the wealthy – fled the city within 48 hours, seeking refuge in their country villas. The plague proved devastating, killing one in every four people. Deaths rose from 48 in July and August to 1,168 in September, and then to 2,121 in October.

This outbreak of bubonic plague had been present in Europe since the previous year. It affected northern Italy, the Grand Duchy of Tuscany and the Republic of Lucca.

In Italy, it became known as the *peste manzoniana*, named after Alessandro Manzoni, who vividly described it in his classic novel *The Betrothed* (*I promessi sposi*) and in his essay *The Infamous Column* (*Storia della colonna infame*). Abroad, it is more commonly referred to as the 'Italian plague'.

PARK OF SACCA SESSOLA

7

A beautiful walk through the park of a former hospital

Island of Sacca Sessola
Accessible via the JW Marriott® Venice Resort's shuttle boat (free), departing every 30 minutes from a private jetty opposite the Giardini Reali

After lying empty for decades, the island of Sacca Sessola has bee brought back to life. A luxury hotel now occupies the centre of park filled with lush vegetation, and everyone is welcome to come fo a stroll.

From 1914 to 1936, the island served as a sanatorium. Then, in 193 a highly modern, cutting-edge respiratory hospital was established. I remained operational until 1979.

An exclusive vegetable garden

Not far from the church, which was built in 1921, a kitchen garden has been created to revive the island's former agricultural identity, producing zero-kilometre vegetables. Even when the island served as a health facility, there was a vegetable garden that supplied the hospital kitchens. The island's particular microclimate creates ideal soil conditions for growing vegetables.

An artificial island created between 1860 and 1870

The name 'Sacca' tells you this island isn't natural. In Venetian terminology, a *sacca* is a man-made island formed by piling up dredged material. It was created between 1860 and 1870 using material excavated during construction of the Santa Marta commercial port. *Sessola* is a dialect word for the tool used to scoop water from boats. The island's shape vaguely resembles it.

NEARBY

The 'Dopolavoro' inscription

'ou can't miss the triking building that nce housed the Dopoavoro – a social centre hat provided workers vith recreational, cultual, sporting and welfare ctivities after working ours.

Now beautifully restoed, it operates as a estaurant.

THE ISLAND OF POVEGLIA

8

A historic island open to visitors once a year

Accessible by private transport only or during events organised by the association Poveglia per Tutti: details available at povegliapertutti.org
Landing is prohibited on the area that once hosted the hospital

The island of Poveglia can be reached only by private transport o during the so-called *Sagranòmala* (see the Facebook page 'Povegli per Tutti').

The island is divided into two distinct areas, separated by a canal: larger section where most of the abandoned buildings are located, and smaller section of natural, wooded areas with no buildings. To the sout of the main island is a third element: a small artificial octagonal islan built for defensive purposes as part of the Venetian lagoon fortification (see p. 205).

Poveglia has ancient origins. In late Roman times, families fleein barbarian invasions from Este, Padua and Monselice took refuge here

The population soon grew enough to form a community governed by a local magistrate, initially called a Gastaldo and later a Podestà. A fortified castle was built, later dismantled in 1379 and replaced with the existing octagonal defensive structure.

The War of Chioggia (1378–1381) brought about the island's ruin, and it was subsequently left uninhabited. In the second half of the 18th century, the island came under the control of the Magistrato della Sanità, which ordered passing ships to carry out repairs here. It was from one of these ships that the plague arrived.

Poveglia then became a new lazaretto, intended for the quarantine of goods and sailors.

Napoleon demolished the church of San Vitale, leaving only the bell tower, which had previously served as a lighthouse, and commissioned the construction of health facilities such as a rest home.

Throughout the 19th century, the island continued to serve a health function, particularly during the cholera epidemics that struck Europe. In the 20th century it was converted into a geriatric sanatorium and was abandoned in 1968.

Sagranòmala

Organised by the association Poveglia per Tutti, which works to restore and reopen the island to the public while opposing its privatisation, the Sagranòmala is held once a year. It offers a range of activities including talks with historians, music, theatrical performances, readings and children's activities. It represents one of the few opportunities for the public to legally visit the island, which is normally off limits.

Since summer 2025, the association has been granted a six-year concession to manage the northern part of Poveglia.

THE POVEGLIA OCTAGON

⑨

A fortification of the Republic of Venice

Island of Poveglia
Accessible by private transport only

The Poveglia Octagon is a fortified artificial islet shaped, as its name suggests, like an octagon. It lies south of Poveglia island in the Venetian Lagoon and forms part of a defensive system of fortifications commissioned by the Republic of Venice from 1571 onwards to protect the city, particularly from the Ottoman threat.

Today, like many of the other octagons, it stands abandoned. No trace of military structures remains – it simply appears as a green island surrounded by a masonry embankment.

The five octagons of the lagoon

The Venetian Lagoon contains five octagons – artificial islands positioned along the access channels, created in the late 16th century for defence. They take their name from their eight-sided shape.

Their purpose was to repel or counter enemy incursions into the lagoon. Today they're mostly abandoned islands, and only the observant eye can detect their original military function.

Starting from the south, the first octagon you encounter is Ca' Roman, which guarded the entrance to the lagoon through the Port of Chioggia. The Port of Malamocco was protected by the San Pietro Octagon and the Alberoni Octagon.

Further north is the Abbandonato Octagon (also called Campana), and lastly the Poveglia Octagon, the oldest of the five. Built in 1380, it served as the model for the others and was strengthened and modernised several times over the centuries.

In 2009, an American television programme called *Ghost Adventures* invented a legend – with no historical foundation whatsoever – about a mad doctor who supposedly performed lobotomies on l'Ottagono di Poveglia and committed suicide by throwing himself from the bell tower.

A bell tower that survived Napoleonic suppressions by serving as a lighthouse

One of the few bell towers remaining in the central lagoon, the Poveglia bell tower is the sole survivor of the vanished church of San Vitale. It features a clock, now without hands, made by Bartolomeo Ferracina in 1745.

Several works from the Church of San Vitale can be seen in the Church of Santa Maria Assunta in Malamocco on the Lido of Venice: a 15th-century plaster and stucco crucifix (see p. 170), two splendid marble groups representing *The Myrrhbearers* by Giuseppe Torretti, and a canvas by Giulia Lama depicting the Virgin in Prayer.

The bell tower survived the Napoleonic suppressions because it was being used as a lighthouse.

THE ISLAND OF FISOLO

⑩

One of eight artificial islets created in the late 1700s for military purposes

Accessible by private transport only

The island of Fisolo lies not far from the Alberoni area and is surrounded by white blocks of Istrian marble that protect its heavily roded embankments. You can reach it by private boat and moor easily, ut take care when going ashore. A few ruins are scattered among the reenery – mainly Second World War bunkers now almost completely wallowed by vegetation.

Fisolo is one of eight artificial islets created towards the end of the 8th century for military use. All eight remained in service until the econd World War, when they were decommissioned and abandoned.

Like the other seven batteries, Fisolo started as a simple pile-dwelling tructure. It was later transformed into a small island and strengthened everal times during the 19th century. The most significant fortifications ere were built in 1881.

The eight artificial islets from the late 1700s: the batteries

Starting from the south, Fisolo is the first artificial islet you'll encounter. Then come Ex Poveglia (not to be confused with the Poveglia octagon), Campana and Trezze. Further north in the lagoon are the batteries of Campalto, Tessera, Carbonera and Buel del Lovo.

Some, including Campana, Trezze and Ex Poveglia, are privately owned. Others belong to the state.

Known as batteries, these islands were crucial for defending Venice from attacks by land and sea, particularly during the Austrian and later Italian periods. They began as simple wooden platforms but were transformed into proper artificial islands with stone fortifications.

Until recently, the central lagoon hosted the Re di Fisolo Regatta – a race for traditional lateen-rigged boats that passed between the islands of Poveglia, Campana and Fisolo.

The name of a bird

The island's name comes from a Venetian dialect word for certain waterfowl, including the little grebe and the gull.

THE LIGHTHOUSE ON SPIGNON ISLAND

11

A tiny island – just 160 square metres – and an old lighthouse protected by the Ministry of Culture

Accessible only by private boat
Can only be visited from the outside; landing is not permitted

At first glance, it's hard to think of Spignon as an island at all but despite its small size – only 160 square metres – it truly is an island

There's an immediate fascination in seeing the remains of th old brick lighthouse, which seems to stand guard over the nearb Malamocco–Marghera Canal – better known as the Canale dei Petroli stretching for 15 km. The island lies not far from the Lido of Venice you can glimpse it while passing by boat or from a walk along the lagoo near the Alberoni district.

The Spignon lighthouse, built in the mid-19th century and now rotected by the Ministry of Culture, is mentioned in documents dating ack to 1886.

The structure, 15 metres tall, together with a few small outbuildings t its base, covers the whole island.

It was once part of a signalling network that included the former lberoni lighthouse and the small Ceppe lighthouse (the only one till in operation), but it was partially decommissioned after the new occhetta lighthouse was completed.

For many years, the buildings served as a storehouse and refuge for assing fishermen.

A refuge for passing recluses?

In 2018, the German company Floatel GmbH, specialist in restoring lighthouses across Europe, was awarded a fifty-year lease on the island, following a tender issued by the State Property Agency and the Ministry of Defence, as part of a project to promote Italian lighthouses. The plan was to transform the site into a retreat for affluent recluses seeking a place for meditation. However, another company (Simerg), which had also taken part in the tender, immediately lodged an appeal with the Regional Administrative Court.

At present, the island is still abandoned.

Where Pius VII moored – the Pope elected on San Giorgio Island in 1800

Historical records indicate that in 1800, the ship Bellona moored for several days near what is now known as Spignon.

On board was Pius VII, born Barnaba Chiaramonti, who was elected Pope on 14 March during the conclave held on the island of San Giorgio (see *Secret Venice* from the same publisher for more details).

After the conclave, Austrian authorities kept the Pope in Venice for nearly three months. When the ship finally headed toward the Adriatic, the captain waited out bad weather before sailing to Pesaro, from which the Pope travelled to Rome by land.

While waiting, the Pontiff visited the island of Pellestrina on 7 June and, two days later, Malamocco.

SHRINE OF THE MADONNA OF THE BOAT-KEEPERS

An ancient maritime tradition

Located on a salt marsh near the channel leading to the Cavane delle Giare
Visible from the boats
Boat procession: late May (around 25 May, from 2pm on)

The lagoon is dotted with shrines, born from the devotion of seafaring people and mostly dedicated to Mary. Stella Maris – Star of the Sea – is one of the Virgin's oldest titles. Like the North Star, she serves as a guide, offering hope and protection to sailors.

In Giare, in the southern lagoon, a shrine stands on the salt marsh beside the *cavane* (covered structures where boats are moored). It symbolically greets and blesses those heading onto the water.

Built in 2018, the shrine was the heartfelt project of the thriving community of *cavanisti* (boat-keepers) who moor their vessels here.

Every year in late May, a procession of boats makes its way to the shrine, where a statue of the Madonna is kept.

The water cortège is accompanied by people walking along the adjacent embankment until they reach the vicinity of boundary marker no.94 (see following double page), from where they can watch the prayer ceremony, albeit from a distance.

The annual procession keeps alive an old tradition of devotion that blends Catholic faith with local folk beliefs – still strong throughout the lagoon.

People come to ask the Madonna for protection when they go out to sea, or to give thanks for surviving danger.

BOUNDARY MARKERS OF GIARE

13

Historic markers showing the boundaries of the Venice Lagoon

Giare area
Starting from Via Cà Nova, follow the cavane (boathouses) heading south, then return towards the centre of the area

While walking in areas bordering land and lagoon, you might notice pillars or small columns in masonry, often made of brick or Istrian stone. Some have a wider base that tapers towards the top.

These structures, numbered and positioned along the perimeter of the Venice Lagoon, mark the legal, administrative and geographical

boundary between the lagoon and the mainland. They represent a widespread monument of great historical and environmental importance.

You'll find nine of these markers, numbered from 92 to 100, walking through the Giare area. Start from Via Cà Nova and follow the boathouses heading south, then loop back towards the centre of the area.

Recently, interest in the markers has been growing, thanks to initiatives aimed at protecting and maintaining these ancient structures.

You can find detailed maps online (restovenezia.it/Cippi%20Home.htm) showing the markers' positions, making it possible to freely organise your own trips to discover them.

Lagoon boundary markers

The term *conterminazione lagunare* (lagoon demarcation) refers to the boundaries of the Venice Lagoon, marked by a series of stone markers. The first plans for this boundary date back to 1600, but the Republic only approved an official line in 1784. Between 1791 and 1792, 99 terracotta markers were erected around the entire perimeter. Many were later replaced with Istrian stone markers during the 19th century. Beyond the main boundary markers, 25 additional ones were placed to mark the edges of three raised areas – the *dossi* of Lugo, Conche and Fogolana. The line was modified in 1924 with a new route that essentially followed the historic one, except in the Brenta delta area, excluding the ancient, raised areas of Conche and Fogolana in the southern lagoon from the perimeter. Following a 1990 decree from the Ministry of Public Works, the route needed updating to reflect natural morphological changes and changes caused by human intervention over previous centuries. The current boundary also includes the three port entrances and the island of Sant'Erasmo which, until 1888 when the Cavallino breakwater was built, wasn't considered an internal lagoon island.

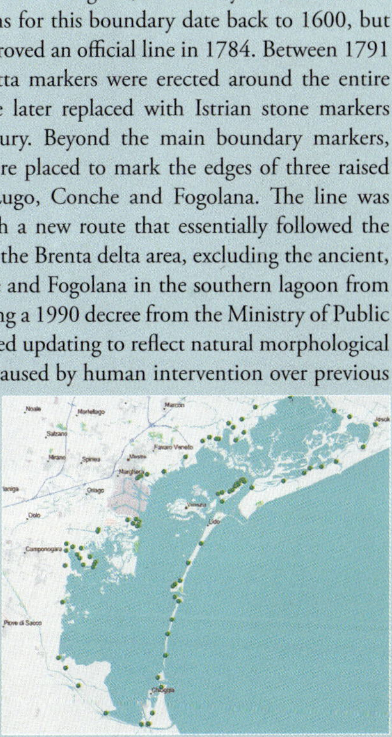

VELO CROSS

(14)

A hidden cross, truly unexpected among fields and salt marshes

Giare, near boundary stone no. 96
Accessible on foot, preferably in autumn or winter

Along a 4-km nature trail – suitable for cycling and walking – near boundary stone no. 96 (see previous double page), a stone marker topped with a cross stands in land surrounded by fields. The inscription at its base reads: 'Homage to Jesus Christ the Redeemer, reverently offered by Domenico and Seconda di Velo, married couple, 17 December 1902'.

Because of the dense vegetation surrounding it, the Velo Cross isn't always accessible. Efforts have been made in the past to clear the path of the various shrubs that blocked approach. It's therefore advisable to visit during autumn or winter months, when the vegetation is subdued.

Probably of German origin, the Velo family takes its name from the fief of Velo d'Astico castle, which it received in 1276 from the then Bishop of Vicenza. Count Domenico di Velo, the landowner, donated the site in Giare in 1894 where the neo-Gothic Church of San Domenico was built (see below).

NEARBY

The spiageta dei puareti

Very close to the Velo Cross, you can see another recently restored spot – the so-called *spiageta dei puareti* ('poor people's beach'), a salt marsh where people who couldn't afford access to the bathing facilities used to swim.

The Oratory of San Domenico

A key part of the locality's history is the Oratory of San Domenico. Its construction was promoted by Don Resh, parish priest of Gambarare from 1887 to 1904, to provide a place of worship for the local community. Built on land donated by Count Velo and begun in 1894, the oratory served as the centre of religious life until 1948, when the Madonna Immacolata nursery school opened with a chapel inside. This new chapel meant the Church of San Domenico was gradually neglected and eventually closed for worship. The oratory was restored and reopened in 2009 through the initiative of Monsignor Luigi Casarin. It has a gabled brick facade and a single-nave interior with exposed beams. During restoration, the original altarpiece (now kept in the rectory of Gambarare's Duomo) was replaced with a new one showing St Dominic receiving a rosary from Mary, with the Giare landscape in the background.

MONUMENT TO ROMEO ISEPETTO

⑮

Remembering a post-war Robin Hood who poached fish to feed the hungry

Giare di Mira area
At the Darsena, always visible
Accessible by private transport only

At Giare, facing the lagoon, three white stones form a simple monument. The top stone bears an inscription carved in bold letters – a memorial to Romeo Isepetto.

Unveiled on 25 April 2015, the monument honours a man whose life was shaped by war, hunger and hardship, and who died in unexplained circumstances.

The inscription on the upper stone reads:
ROMEO ISEPETTO BORN IN TREPORTI – BURANO 24 JANUARY 1897

FISHERMAN. COMMUNIST. PARTISAN
HE DREAMED THAT THE LAGOON WOULD RETURN TO BEING COMMON PROPERTY WHEN
FISH BELONGED TO THOSE WHO CAUGHT IT TO LIVE AND LET OTHERS LIVE
IN THESE VALLEYS HE MET HIS DEATH
WITH HIS FISHING COMPANION GIUSEPPE FABBIAN ON 17 AUGUST 1947
IN MEMORY OF HIM. ERECTED BY THE GIUSEPPE ISEPETTO COMMITTEE
GIARE DI MIRA – 14 SEPTEMBER 2014

Born in Treporti, Isepetto moved with his family to Mira in 1928. During the war, he became a riverside partisan, helping free English prisoners from the Giare di Mira camp.

On 9 September 1943, he led the first non-violent partisan action in Mira – occupying the town hall with a small group. He was arrested, imprisoned in Dolo, then hastily moved to Venice to prevent local unrest.

The following summer, he was sent to Mauthausen concentration camp. When he returned in June 1945, he weighed just 46 kg.

Back in Mira, he stood alongside workers striking at Mira Lanza, the historic soap and detergent factory. He founded a fishing cooperative whose members often poached in the valleys using homemade explosives – crude bombs containing unstable calcium carbide.

They shared their daily catch with struggling families. This earned him his reputation as a post-war Robin Hood.

On 17 August 1947, Isepetto died alongside his friend Bepi Fabbian when one of these explosives went off as they fished in the marshes. Some still believe his death was no accident.

A year after the monument's unveiling, musicians Gualtiero Bertelli and Moira Mion told his story in *Ballata di Romeo Isepetto*.

BETTONI GRASSI ORATORY

(16)

A small Madonna rediscovered in a little-known place of great charm

Via Argine dx Novissimo
Località Porto Menai - Mira (VE)
Accessible by private transport only

If you find yourself near Porto Menai in the municipality of Mira, you'll be captivated by what remains of the Bettoni Grassi Oratory. Its neoclassical facade reflected in the water captures the essence of a little-known but deeply atmospheric place.

Located in an area rich with history, the oratory is linked to the ›resence of the River Medoacus Maior (later known as a branch of he Brenta) and an ancient port that allowed the people of Padua, and ›thers, to reach the port of Malamocco on the Lido of Venice.

In 1740, the Bettoni family bought a villa as a weekend residence rom the Agapito family, who had owned the property since 1625.

The building therefore became known as Villa Bettoni, and from ›atriarchal visits to the Gambarare area we know there was already an ›ratory connected to the villa, dedicated to St Charles.

However, Monsignor Federico Maria Giovannelli's 1780 report nentions an oratory dedicated to the Holy Trinity instead. The lack ›f more precise documentation leaves doubt as to whether this was the ame building.

In 1808, the villa appears in the Napoleonic Cadastre as a holiday .ome owned by Angela Bettoni, the widow of Signor Grassi, who was ›uried here when she died in 1817. She left the oratory to Antonio ₹ota, a pricst, and Domenico Pujati.

In 1880, a flood from a breach in the Novissimo canal embankment ɛft the property in a dangerous state, and it was demolished. Until that ›oint, the oratory had been used not only by its owners but also by local ›eople who could attend services there.

Only the facade of the building survived, as recorded on a plaque ɛt into the central doorway of the structure. The facade bears two ıscriptions, one on the pediment and one on the doorway lintel.

Restoration of the portal, carried out by the Mira Local Heritage Committee, was inaugurated in June 2011. For the occasion, a copy had een made of the little Madonna statue that mysteriously disappeared lmost 25 years earlier.

Professor Clauco Benito Tiozzo created the replacement, cast in ronze using the lost-wax method, based on an old photograph of the riginal. But on the morning of 2 May, the unthinkable happened: vorkers found the riginal statue near the ite. It was returned to s place and can now e admired there. On ıat occasion, Angela Bettoni's remains were ansferred to Gambarare Cemetery.

THE 'IDROFORO' INSCRIPTION

17

A reminder of the building that brought drinking water to Venice

Via Pallada, Fusina (VE)
Accessible by private transport only

From the Moranzani locks (see following double page), head sout along Via Pallada, then take the road to the right. Along the wa you'll spot a building now converted into a private house, bearing th inscription IDROFORO.

This 19th-century structure was built to supply Venice with drinkin water, operating in conjunction with a cast-iron aqueduct that used t

ın beneath the lagoon at the time. Until that time, drinking water :ached the city by barge, so the construction of this building between 882 and 1883 represented a major breakthrough.

Inside, a pumping system drew water from the Seriola Canal. After urification, the water was pumped into a large reservoir in Venice at ant'Andrea, then distributed to homes. It was a remarkable feat of ıechanical engineering, cutting-edge for its time.

The structure was divided into three sections: a basement housing ırbines, a ground floor with machinery and sluice gates, and a first oor with the keeper's quarters.

Sadly, today the building is recognisable only by its large inscription. 'races of the purification tanks and other external elements can only be :en from the air.

Even now, a significant portion of Venice's water network, including :ctions beneath the lagoon, consists of cast-iron pipes dating from the ıte 19th century. These century-old pipes demonstrate the engineering uality of the era but require constant maintenance.

Renovation and replacement of some old pipes got under way in 025, introducing new materials (such as steel) and more modern :chniques to ensure efficient and safe water supply for Venice's future. . recent example is the installation of two new pipes beneath the ıgoon, parallel to the Ponte della Libertà, to strengthen the network 'om Tronchetto.

NEARBY

Bosco Moranzani

:ontinue along the road and shortly after, on your left, you'll find Bosco Aoranzani, an agricultural area becoming Italy's first forest designed to e fully accessible and inclusive.

'lanted in 2022, the first tree will eventually be part of a forest housing ,300 new native trees and shrubs of 17 different species.

'he project aims to create an area accessible to everyone. During the ılanning phase, all possible barriers were removed and services and ctivities were designed to meet the various needs.

'he area will feature a cycle and pedestrian path enhanced with benches, ignage and tactile Braille paths.

'he growing forest will also bring environmental benefits: reduced :O2, mitigation of climate change effects and increased biodiversity.

TOLL PLAQUE AT MORANZANI LOCK

A transit point with 17th-century toll rates carved in stone

Via Moranzani, Fusina (VE)
Bus: line 16

At Malcontenta, in the Moranzani area, you'll find a lock consisting of an oval basin with white stone walls that solved a practical problem – the height difference between the lagoon and the River Brenta.

On the facade of the lock-keeper's house, two inscriptions from Venetian Republic days still list the toll charges for passing boats. The rates varied depending on the cargo's value and where it came from.

Some goods were exempt from tolls altogether. These included cargo from Gambarare, which belonged to the ancient Dogado, and boats travelling from Venice to Moranzan specifically to process wool before returning to the city.

These strict regulations are preserved in the two inscriptions mentioned above, one of which details the various tariffs in force.

Before locks were introduced, the height difference between the Brenta and the lagoon was managed using the so-called Fusina Cart – a contraption consisting of two wooden platforms and two stone rails.

Boats were hauled between lagoon and river using a rope wound round a rotating beam, which was turned by a toothed wheel mechanism powered by animals. The Fusina Cart was demolished on 22 March 1611 and replaced by locks built at Mira.

NEARBY

The old Moranzani locks

Via Pallada, Fusina (VE)

It seems almost impossible that next to Porto Marghera's vast industrial plants lies such a distinctive ancient site – the Moranzani lock, where boats once stopped to pay tolls for passage along the Naviglio Brenta between Venice and Padua.

Written records, maps and paintings all bear witness to its importance as more than just a crossing point.

Soon after this and other locks were built along the Brenta, stopping places sprang up for travellers – spots where people could refresh themselves, exchange gossip and trade goods informally.

Built in 1602 to overcome the level difference between the canal, then called Brenta Secca, and the lagoon, it came into operation before 1613, when the Fusina Cart was dismantled (see above).

This ancient lock, no longer in use, once connected the lagoon with the Bodante di Sotto canal and is now known as the old Moranzani locks.

Though somewhat hidden, half-guarded by vegetation and water, it's still visible if you know where to look.

VENEZIA HERITAGE TOWER

19

Europe's only cooling tower transformed into a cultural and exhibition centre

Corso Gianni Sottana
Marghera (VE)
0329 6344218 – veneziaheritagetower.com
Opening hours vary, check website
Accessible by private transport only

Within the port and industrial complex of Marghera stands th spectacular Venezia Heritage Tower, a former evaporative coolin

:ower in reinforced concrete built in 1938.

Of the five cooling towers constructed in Marghera during that period, :his is the only one still standing.

For years it cooled enormous quantities of boiling water from the processing operations in the area's large industrial plants. In 1923, Giovanni Agnelli (legendary founder of FIAT, Fabbrica Italiana Automobili Torino) commissioned architect Vittorio Bonadè Bottino to oversee the construction of a flat glass production plant in the Marghera area. Here, the glass manufacturing company Vetrocoke operated alongside other industries, with Agnelli serving as its president until 1945.

The tower is now called Venezia Heritage Tower and is often known by its initialism, VHT.

Owned by the Consorzio Multimodale Darsena, the structure was the brainchild of entrepreneur Gianni Sottana. The name was chosen because 'heritage' in English means both inheritance and cultural legacy.

Extensive and careful restoration has transformed an abandoned and deteriorating site into a multi-purpose centre – the only example in Europe of a water cooling tower converted into a cultural and exhibition hub.

Inside, roughly 3,000 square metres spread across six floors house various spaces, including a conference hall and a museum trail featuring a permanent exhibition dedicated to the industrial achievements that marked Porto Marghera's history.

An extraordinary panoramic observatory

The top floor houses 'the observatory', which offers sweeping 360-degree views. You can see Venice and its lagoon, the Euganean Hills and the Alps, but most significantly, Marghera's industrial landscape spread out below – a living testament to over a century of industrial history, revealing stories that deserve to be understood and explored.

A masterpiece of industrial archaeology

The original form (hyperboloid) of this genuine masterpiece of industrial archaeology, standing nearly 60 metres tall with a diameter of 28 metres at the base and 21 metres at the summit, was designed by engineer Giuseppe Colombo, who adapted a Franco–Dutch project.

Southern Lagoon

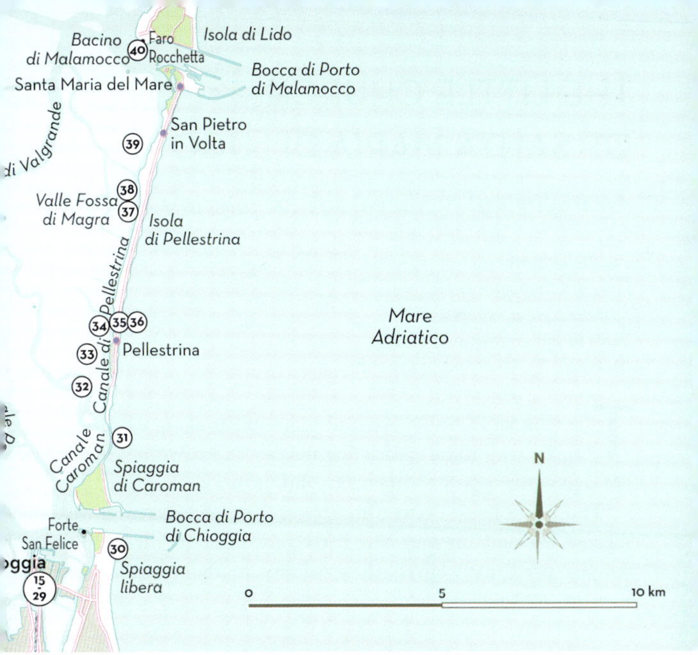
Isola di Lido
Bacino
di Malamocco
Faro
Rocchetta
Bocca di Porto
di Malamocco
Santa Maria del Mare
San Pietro
in Volta
Valle Fossa
di Magra
Isola
di Pellestrina
Canale di Pellestrina
Pellestrina
Mare
Adriatico
Canale
Caroman
Spiaggia
di Caroman
Bocca di Porto
di Chioggia
Forte
San Felice
Spiaggia
libera
N
0
5
10 km

THE LITTLE CHURCH OF SANTA MARIA DI LUGO

①

An important medieval site for pilgrims and art

Via Pio la Torre
Lugo di Campagna Lupia
comune.campagnalupia.ve.it
Visits by appointment only
Accessible by private transport only

The Church of Santa Maria di Lugo stands along what was once a crucial river route connecting the city and territory of Padua with the lagoon, the port of Malamocco and the sea.

The name Lugo derives from *lucus*, meaning sacred grove, which suggests the building may have been constructed on the site of a pagan temple, particularly given its proximity to the consular road from Ravenna to Aquileia.

However, this theory remains unproven.

What we do know is that in 1399 the church was a stopping point for the White Penitents movement, a penitential group from Umbria that travelled in procession from one place of worship to another.

In the 14th century, during the territorial disputes between Venice and Padua, the church was joined to the Sacristy of Padua Cathedral, as recorded on a plaque on the left wall of the presbytery.

Evidence that this was a pilgrimage site comes from a 1438 papal document: Pope Eugene IV granted indulgences to those who visited the church between 8 and 13 September.

On the south-east walls, some stone corbels probably supported a roof that provided shelter for the many pilgrims.

Inside, on the left, stands an 18th-century altar moved from the presbytery, with a precious marble inlay depicting a Pietà.

It was once adorned with a wooden statue of the Madonna Addolorata (Our Lady of Sorrows), stolen in 1966 and recovered in Umbria in 2019.

LOVA PUMPING STATION

(2)

One of the symbols of the history of land reclamation in the Venetian region

Via Giacomo Leopardi, 1
30010 Campagna Lupia (VE)
consorzio@acquerisorgive.it
Accessible by private transport only
Group visits available by prior arrangement with the Acque Risorgive Land Reclamation Consortium

Built between 1890 and 1895, the Lova pumping station is undoubtedly one of the most significant symbols of land reclamation in the Venetian area.

Pumping stations like this, scattered along the lagoon's edge, have always played – and still play – a vital role: they mechanically lift water

from reclaimed areas and ensure the drainage of land lying below sea level or prone to flooding.

The Republic of Venice always paid particular attention to its waters. Over the centuries, it carried out numerous modifications to river courses, mouths and lagoon canals to protect this delicate environment.

In the 16th century, following various works to close and divert rivers flowing into the lagoon, the inland areas repeatedly flooded.

To address this, the Sette Prese del Brenta – public consortia created to manage all the waters flowing from the countryside into a single hydraulic system – were established on 23 June 1604. From these arose today's modern Land Reclamation Consortia.

The water lifted here is channelled into the lagoon through a holding basin, serving the towns of Campolongo Maggiore, Piove di Sacco, Campagna Lupia, Camponogara and Dolo.

Originally equipped with two steam-powered turbine pumps, the station was modernised in 1912 with the installation of a diesel-driven centrifugal pump.

About a decade later, in 1922–23, with the arrival of electricity, one of the steam pumps was replaced by an electric centrifugal pump, and in 1964, the second steam pump was also replaced with a new model.

The plant has been continuously updated to keep pace with modern technology and improve its effectiveness.

Today, the Lova pumping station stands as a true example of industrial archaeology, still housing a three-cylinder diesel engine dating back almost a century.

MUSEUM OF DRAINAGE PUMPS AT CODEVIGO

3

A museum about the history of land reclamation

Via Idrovora - Santa Margherita di Codevigo (PD)
info@consorziobacchiglione.it
Visits by appointment only
Accessible by private transport only

The historic drainage pump station at Santa Margherita stands in the countryside just a few hundred metres from the lagoon, on a strip of land that, were it not for the pumps, would frequently flood and be left unusable and uninhabitable.

The plant has existed for over a century, remains fully operational and plays a vital role for the areas covering the municipalities of Piove di Sacco, Arzergrande, Pontelongo, Correzzola and Codevigo.

The complex not only functions but also houses a museum documenting the history of land reclamation.

The first pump system comprised a paddle wheel 11 metres in diameter, built in 1888 and powered by a steam engine. It was demolished in 1963 and replaced with two centrifugal pumps driven by a diesel engine.

In 1898, the plant was expanded with a second engine room, and two turbines powered by a steam engine were installed. The turbines were replaced in 1954 with two centrifugal pumps driven by a diesel engine, which was in turn superseded by an electric motor.

Finally, in 1911, two further centrifugal pumps were installed in a third engine room, initially operating with producer gas engines and, from 1917, with electric motors.

The old coal store now serves as a documentation centre, housing a documentary and photographic archive along with countless historical films. The museum features a working scale model of the historic paddle wheel to demonstrate the mechanism to visitors.

This example of industrial archaeology tells the story of a landscape shaped and preserved by human intervention. As a plaque on the plant's facade records, thanks to the Baccarini Law of 1882, the state intervened with public works to improve Italy's geological conditions, implementing a vast drainage programme that also defeated malaria.

THE PROCESSION OF THE GREEN ④ MADONNA OF SANTA MARGHERITA DI CODEVIGO

An unknown tradition that is renewed every year on the first Sunday in October

The original statue is located in the Church of Saints Felice and Fortunato in Santa Margherita di Codevigo
Piazza Santi Felice e Fortunato, 2
35020 Codevigo (Pd)
Every first Sunday in October, in the afternoon

Almost unknown, but very characteristic, is the procession held every first Sunday in October in the countryside of the hamlet of Santa Margherita di Codevigo, dedicated to a Madonna who, according to legend, arrived from the Lagoon.

According to tradition, the statue arrived by sea, enclosed in a marble niche, and ran aground in a place where there is now a farm (near the so-called Corte Fogolana), but which in ancient times was lapped by water.

The story goes that the people wanted to take it to the church of Brenta dell'Abbà (a hamlet of Correzzola, in the province of Padua), but while crossing the Bacchiglione river, the boat suddenly became very heavy and was in danger of sinking. It was therefore believed that the Madonna did not want to cross the river, so they turned back and the statue miraculously became light again.

Some sources suggest that the image of the Virgin Mary had also been carried in procession by the faithful in the past and that it was covered when rain was invoked and uncovered when good weather was requested.

Evidence of this custom can be found in the veil kept in the church dedicated to Saints Felice and Fortunato in Santa Margherita di Codevigo, where the original statue is also located, a copy of which is carried in procession.

The procession, which is about three kilometres long and was revived in 1999 after many years thanks to Don Renato Galiazzo, takes place strictly on foot and is followed by a large community. The cart is decorated with pomegranates, shells and seasonal fruits, and the starting point is decorated with ribbons and large banners bearing prayers for the Immaculate Conception.

In addition to the manner of its miraculous discovery, which it shares with other sacred icons found in a similar way (such as the Madonna of Marina di Malamocco or the Madonna of Caorle), the peculiarity of this work lies in the discovery, after restoration, of the true colour of its mantle, which was blue. Under a layer of paint, it was discovered, to everyone's surprise, that the Virgin's veil was originally green.

CASONI DELLA FOGOLANA

5

UNESCO World Heritage casoni

Via Cason delle Sacche, 8
Codevigo (PD)
Accessible by private transport only
Park open Saturdays and Sundays from 9am to 6pm

Declared a UNESCO World Heritage Site, the casoni della Fogolana are recently constructed buildings that recreate the typical dwellings of the Saccisica countryside.

The roof is conical and made of straw, while the masonry sections are built from sun-baked bricks.

While the interiors are closed for maintenance, the surrounding park is open and can be freely explored.

By the late 15th century, the countryside *casone* already had a well-defined form: rectangular or square floor plan, perimeter walls in masonry, and a roof of marsh reeds with very steep slopes, plus a small door and balcony.

Its defining feature is the roof, formed from bundles of marsh reed and wheat straw arranged on a wooden frame to create sloping surfaces that channel rainwater away.

The orientation of the dwelling was crucial to ensure warmth and light. Knowledge of the prevailing winds also guaranteed proper chimney draw, otherwise, sparks could easily set the roof ablaze.

The rooms were arranged in a spiral. From the entrance you'd access the kitchen, the stable and the bedrooms, which typically ranged from one to four.

Casoni were never more than one storey high, though the loft space, usually used as a hayloft, could sometimes be lived in.

The main roof beam was made of poplar. In the Padua area, it was customary to plant one of these trees at the birth of each son, so that by the time of his marriage there would be a tree of suitable size to expand the family home.

Later, however, the trunks forming the main roof structure came from spruce and other conifers, which were imported from the Dolomites thanks to the Serenissima's trading networks.

Despite later developments, these remained humble structures built from simple materials, their design clearly inspired by the hunting and fishing huts found in the valleys.

The Paduan casoni reflect a new chapter in land use, one shaped by drainage works and the growth of agriculture that followed.

Today they've almost completely disappeared. No more than seven remain in the Padua area: four have been restored and recovered and are located in the municipality of Piove di Sacco; one is in the Ethnographic Park in Rubano; and two others are in Arzergrande and Conselve respectively.

CASONE DELLE SACCHE

⑥

From hunters' lodge to ecomuseum

Via Cason Delle Sacche
Codevigo (PD)
villaroberti.com
Open Saturdays and Sundays: 11am–5.30pm, closed in bad weather
For opening times and further information: casonesacche@villaroberti.com
Accessible by private transport only

The casone delle Sacche sits on a strip of land in the Valle Millecampi, on what's known as the island of Fogolana. Its name comes from its location facing a *sacca* – a lagoon inlet that extends into the surrounding countryside.

Built in 1874, it originally provided accommodation for hunters, mostly from the Paduan hinterland. A valley keeper accompanied them on shoots, ensuring hunts stayed within the rules and territorial boundaries.

After years lying empty, the building was carefully restored. Since 2008 it has housed the Millecampi Ecomuseum, which promotes understanding of the local area.

Information panels throughout the site explain the history, flora and fauna of the surroundings.

One particularly useful panel outlines six routes through Codevigo's cultural landscape and neighbouring areas, on foot, by bike or on horseback.

In 2025, an association took over management of the casone. They open it at weekends and organise cultural events.

Inside, a large ground-floor room has been recreated to show how people lived in traditional lagoon casoni.

You can also climb the spiral staircase to the top of the observation tower for views across the surrounding landscape.

A Dino Risi film with Marcello Mastroianni and Sophia Loren

The casone featured in the 1971 film *La moglie del prete* (*The Priest's Wife*) by director Dino Risi, starring Marcello Mastroianni and Sophia Loren.

In the film, it's the home of Mastroianni's character's parents – he plays a priest.

A poster for the film is displayed on the ground floor.

ABANDONED CEMETERY OF CONCHE

⑦

The dead saved the living

Conche (PD), Via Zena
Open for the flood commemoration on 4 November, or the Sunday following 4 November
The interior can be viewed through two gates
Accessible by private transport only

A grey fence runs the length of the site, interrupted only by a short brick wall behind which stands a small chapel. Through two gates you can glimpse what remains of what was once a cemetery.

Conche lies in the municipality of Codevigo, the same area known for the thatched houses of Fogolana, Valle Millecampi, the Sacche house and Boschettona Beach. In the Zena district, near the River Brenta, this abandoned cemetery stands as witness to an extraordinary night that marked the village forever – yet miraculously took no lives.

On 4 November 1966, the Venice tides reached 194 cm above mean sea level. Pellestrina was evacuated. At around 9pm, the River Brenta burst through its left bank near Conche, sending floodwater cascading across the countryside between river and lagoon.

The surge swept towards the village with devastating force, but the cemetery stood directly in its path, breaking the wave's power and slowing its advance. The water completely devastated the small cemetery. Many burial vaults collapsed and coffins began floating across the fields. In the days that followed, bodies were recovered up to 3 km away. Some were even found in the lagoon.

People quickly realised the cemetery had saved Conche from destruction. Contemporary accounts record a deeply moving observation: 'The dead saved the living'.

A new cemetery was built. All the deceased still present in the flood-damaged graveyard were moved there. Those recovered from the surrounding countryside were laid to rest in a communal grave. The cemetery that had taken the full force of the flood was declared a 'Monument to Memory'.

Today, inside the fence, you can still see fragments of family tombs, empty burial vaults and headstones carefully stacked and preserved.

BOSCHETTONA BEACH

(8)

A lagoon beach that's part of the UNESCO World Heritage Site 'Venice and its Lagoon'

Via Valcittadella, 33
35020 Codevigo (PD)
Open all year
Accessible by private transport only

Located in the municipality of Codevigo, in the Valle Millecampi area, Boschettona Beach is officially part of the UNESCO World Heritage Site 'Venice and its Lagoon'. It isn't on the Mediterranean Sea, but on the lagoon itself, and is the only beach in the province of Padua.

As its name suggests – 'Boschettona' hints at a small woodland – the area was once covered by a forest, which was cleared in the early 1900s and originally stretched across about 70 fields.

You reach the beach via an unpaved road, typical of those in the area, passing fields now turned to farmland. Along the way, you can spot the ruins of what was once the traditional *casone*, known as the Boschettona.

There are no beach umbrellas or bathing facilities here – just walkways that let you enjoy an almost untouched landscape, perfect for birdwatching, and a favourite spot for kitesurfers, thanks to the steady winds for much of the year.

It's a little corner of paradise, home to typical coastal plants and, if you're lucky, you might spot the famous pink flamingos that have been visiting the lagoon for years.

CASONE MILLECAMPI

9

The charm of two particularly evocative places

Municipality of Codevigo
Accessible only by water and with private transport
Not open to visitors, but can be circumnavigated

Valle Millecampi is a vast area located at the southern end of the Venetian Lagoon, covering approximately 2,200 km², of which about 1,600 are in the province of Padua, in the municipality of Codevigo. To the north and east, the valley borders the municipalities of Campagna Lupia and Chioggia, in the province of Venice. The current appearance of the valley is the result of hydraulic reorganisation carried out by the Republic of Venice from the end of the 16th century onwards, and the subsequent management of the area as an open/semi-enclosed fishing valley. Casone Millecampi is located at the eastern end of the valley, on the mound of the same name. Clearly dating back to the Renaissance, it is an early example of the evolution of the casone towards a stable brick structure. These buildings were usually made of reeds and straw, as N.H. Pietro Duodo di Chioggia reminds us in a report dated 3 November 1654, in which he reported that the valley had several owners who rented it to a company of Vallesani. The report states that the valley was dotted with several straw casoni, built right on top of the salt marsh. Reaching the fishing sites was never easy, due to the tidal flow, which made navigation impossible when the water was at its lowest. For decades, the journeys were dangerous and long, so much so that 'floating villages' had to be built. Alongside these structures, masonry buildings were constructed to provide more effective shelter from the elements: these were the huts, where the *Capo Valle* (valley chief) often lived.

At the beginning of the 19th century, the Casone Millecampi was a large building with a solid masonry structure, whose base was partially composed of *altinelle* (small huts) around which other smaller buildings stood. Completely restored and rebuilt in recent times, it can only be reached by boat and is recognisable by its large Vallesana-style chimney, typical of fishing valleys. Until the 1950s, this area was home to many workers who harvested and tied the reeds into bundles.

To transport them from Casone Millecampi to Casone delle Sacche (see p. 240), which was closer to the mainland, walkways were created by inserting poles into the seabed, and the reeds were carried on the shoulders or with wheelbarrows. The two casoni are only a few kilometres apart as the crow flies, but the walkways, following the salt marshes, made the journey much longer. The most courageous made the journey by bicycle.

THE RUINS OF CASONE PRIME POSTE

⑩

The brick building that 'rises' from the water

Municipality of Campagna Lupia
Southern Lagoon
Accessible by private transport only

In the municipality of Campagna Lupia, accessible only at high tide and with your own transport, the ruins of Casone Prime Poste seem to rise from the water, almost like a mirage.

Fishermen recall that around 1960, although unsafe, the building was mostly intact, with its two floors still clearly visible. The building was called *Prime Poste* because it was used by fishermen as the first place to process their catch, store their boats and keep their equipment.

In 2020, the Casone Prime Poste was the subject of an interesting project that evaluated the possibility of constructing a modern building while maintaining the existing structures, obviously restoring them. The aim would be to create a charming and highly original place where visitors can soak up the atmosphere of this particular area of the lagoon, observing the movements and activities of the bird species.

This evocative place appears in Carlo Mazzacurati's film *La lingua del santo* (2000), starring Fabrizio Bentivoglio and Antonio Albanese, inspired by the theft of the relic of St Anthony of Padua's chin in 1991.
The film was shot in Padua, the Euganean Hills and the Venetian lagoon, and in some shots you can see the casone in the background.

Casone Millecampi

Typical structures of the lagoon's fishing valleys

To understand how a fishing valley works, it helps to look at the typical structures found within it – each designed for a specific purpose, and all essential to the smooth running of fish farming. Among the most important are *gorghi* and *peschiere*: circular pools about 10–15 metres in diameter, or small stretches of water enclosed by inner embankments.

These are used to house young fish – known as fry – during the first months of rearing, keeping them safe and allowing them to grow, protected from possible predators.

The *peschiere di sverno* (wintering ponds) are made up of parallel basins, several metres wide and varying in length.

Their depth, and the shelter offered by windbreaks or hedges, help maintain temperatures slightly higher at the bottom than at the surface. In winter, any fish that have been caught but are not yet large enough for market are kept in these ponds.

The peschiere are usually covered with nets to keep out herons and cormorants.

Another key feature is the main *chiavica* – a masonry structure, usually with vertically operated sluice gates, which allows salt water from the lagoon to be let into the fishing valley.

The main chiavica is especially important in autumn, as it allows seawater to be brought in.

This encourages fish to migrate for breeding and guides them towards the *lavorieri* – the large basins used for catching them.

You'll also come across *cavane* in the lagoon: these are typical stilted shelters for boats and equipment.

Built with sturdy piles sunk into the water, they have a sloping roof, are closed on three sides, and open directly onto the canal to allow boats to come and go easily.

The hunting casòn

The *casòn di caccia* generally serves as the guesthouse where the owners of the valley and their guests stay during hunting days. It's here that historic collections of trophies and weapons are usually kept. These are often grand buildings, sometimes true lagoon villas. Worthy of special mention are the well-known Casone di Valle Zappa – famous for its Northern European architectural style (see p. 254) – and the Casòn Labia in Valle Figheri, whose facade features a large sundial decorated with representations of the 12 zodiac signs. Guests would usually arrive at the casòn the day before the hunt. Evenings were spent in good company and, most importantly, planning the most effective hunting strategies with the *capo valle* (head of the valley). After, there would be a draw for the shooting positions, known as *botti*.

These botti were wooden structures, set either on dry land or entirely in the water, often near a *coveja* – a patch of reeds used to hide the boat during the hunt.

From autumn through spring, the main quarry from these valley hunts was wildfowl: ducks, mallards, wigeon, pintails and pochards. Starting in 1888, to protect local wildlife, the Provincial Council introduced the first restrictions on the hunting season, which would end in late April and resume in mid-August.

Other structures typically found near, or as part of the casòn, included *altane* or *specole*: raised towers for watching migratory birds between September and January.

These were generally sturdy towers with staircases leading up to heights of 10 metres or more. From these vantage points, using binoculars, the composition of bird flocks could be observed and reported to the head gamekeeper.

Valle Figheri and Valle Zappa still have cylindrical altane towers where you can take in views of the surrounding landscape, and it's not unusual to come across ruins of other such structures, or to find some that have been carefully restored.

A fishing casòn

A *casòn di pesca* is a building where the head of the valley (*capo valle*) and the workers (*vallesani*) who manage the fishing valley live and work. These buildings vary in style but are generally simple and functional in design. Some, however, are surprisingly elegant – solid, square structures that almost look like noble villas. Notable examples can be seen in Valle di Grassabò, Valle Dogà and Valle Dragojesolo in the northern part of the lagoon, and in Valle Averto in the south.

A distinctive feature of fishing and hunting casoni is the chimney – a large, traditional chimney, typical of lagoon architecture, rising above a semicircular, square, or octagonal hearth that juts out from the building's profile.

According to tradition, on autumn and winter evenings, staff would gather around these hearths after dinner, settling onto the wooden benches that surround the fire to enjoy the classic Venetian *filò* – an evening of storytelling and conversation.

If you walk along the bank of the Cornio canal, you can still see the remains of the old casòn of Valle Averto, with its impressive chimney.

Next to the casòn di pesca, you'll usually find outbuildings where all the equipment needed to run the valley is stored.

Some of these spaces have been turned into small ethnographic museums dedicated to traditional lagoon fish farming, preserving the humble, hidden spirit of the old vallesani who often devoted their entire working lives to the valley.

In more recent times, these buildings have been adapted to house cold rooms and facilities for preparing fish destined for the markets.

Fishing valleys of the southern lagoon ⑪

The *valli da pesca*, or fishing valleys, are in the most sheltered parts of the northern and southern parts of the lagoon, in what's known as the *gronda* – the strip of land where the lagoon meets the mainland characterised by islets, mudflats, sandbanks and winding channels.

These areas are used for *vallicoltura*, or extensive fish farming.

Documents, particularly from the 11th century onwards, show that ownership of these fishing valleys was limited to a handful of noble families and Benedictine monasteries. Generally, they were managed through yearly lease agreements, renewed on a regular basis.

There were, however, cases where leases were granted for much longer periods.

The tenancy contracts for these valleys set out the manager's responsibility not only for fish farming but also for building embankments and ditches to protect the land, along with other works to safeguard the lagoon environment.

Expenses for these works were reimbursed by the Venetian authorities.

These valleys weren't just for raising fish – hunting also took place here, an activity which, for the Republic of Venice, provided an important source of food in times of need.

CASONE OF VALLE ZAPPA

⑫

The most distinctive building in the southern lagoon, once frequented by Ernest Hemingway and Salvador Dalí

Valle Zappa - Campagna Lupia
Private property, visible from the canal outside, occasionally open to the public
Accessible by private transport or guided tours

The Casone of Valle Zappa is spectacular and features a Nordic-style building constructed between 1923 and 1928 to designs by architect Duilio Torres.

This complex stands out not only for its truly distinctive form, which nevertheless sits in perfect harmony with its surroundings, but also for the colours of the buildings.

All the structures – both the terracotta sections and the woodwork – are painted in multiple colours that resist the salt air, while decorative motifs and natural imagery embellish the whole.

The broad, sloping roofs echo those typical of the Alpine valleys.

The interior of the main building was created with the same attention as the exterior, with each guest room painted a different colour. During hunting parties, each guest was assigned the colour of their room.

On the house facade hangs a coat of arms depicting three spades: the symbol of the Arrigoni degli Oddi family, who owned the valley from 1867 to 1942.

A plaque records that, between August 1877 and December 1921, the Honourable Count E. Arrigoni degli Oddi shot 51,303 birds with an exceptional average of 62 birds per outing.

The main building and barn are surrounded by a garden with numerous plant species and many fruit trees.

Various notable figures have visited the casone, including Ernest Hemingway and Salvador Dalí. It is said that the latter was responsible for adding several small windows to the building.

The complex also includes a small building nearby, probably a sort of watchtower or guardhouse, with a small statue of the Madonna on top of the roof.

You can reach the top of the tower, used for spotting game, via an external spiral staircase.

THE RUINS OF CASONE BARENON ⑬

The unknown story of Jewish families hidden in the casone

Location: Valle de Bon – Municipality of Campagna Lupia (VE)
Accessible by private boat, visible only from the outside: landing on the islet is prohibited

Built between 1810 and 1840, Casone Barenon is a discreet witness and silent guardian of a history that has long remained unknown.

All that remains is the outline of an old fireplace, a few scattered ruins, traces of a life lived that recall the charm of living – almost hermit-like – in the fishing valleys of the South Lagoon, in years when time still passed slowly, with rhythms often dictated by climatic and meteorological conditions.

It was here that, during the Second World War, Cencio Doria, known as Fofe, a fisherman from Chioggia who had moved to Marghera, risked

his life to hide several Jewish families, who then fled to Switzerland and thus escaped Nazi-Fascist persecution, as well as partisans from the Vittorino Boscolo Fiore brigade.

This story has only recently come to light, thanks to the memories of Erminia Doria Pandin, daughter of the courageous Cencio, who lived at Casone Barenon for over a year and a half, until late spring 1945, when the terrible conflict came to an end.

Erminia recalled how some of her uncles, fearing discovery and execution by the Germans, did not agree with these initiatives, but Cencio prevailed due to his age and insisted on continuing this work of solidarity.

These memories were collected by Ermes Pandin, known as Meme, Erminia's son and Cencio's grandson, who created a theatrical performance entitled "Al Barenon... Anime in guerra" (At Barenon... Souls at War).

The island is surrounded by shallow waters, making it quite difficult to approach. Furthermore, landing is prohibited.

The legend of the Valley of the Seven Dead Men (14)

Between Chioggia and Venice, roughly opposite Pellestrina in the southern lagoon, lies an area known as the Valley of the Seven Dead Men. The legend of the valley of the seven dead men is an old fishermen's tale, told in various forms along the Venetian coastline in places like Chioggia, Pellestrina, Grado and Muggia. The main characters are seven fishermen, later joined by a young boy. The legend has it that the fishermen ignored the superstition that forbids fishing on the Night of the Dead (from 1 to 2 November) and set out to sea. As they hauled in their nets, they discovered the body of a man tangled in the catch. When they pulled the corpse aboard, a sudden storm struck, forcing them to seek shelter in a brightly lit casòn (a traditional fisherman's hut). Inside, they found a boy with his dog. When dinner was ready, the fishermen decided to play a trick on the boy and sent him to fetch their companion, who had stayed in the boat. Unaware, the boy went out and called for the companion several times but, of course, no one answered. But eventually, he returned to the hut with the man, who had come

back to life. The seven fishermen, terrified, died instantly and, the next morning, their bodies were found in the hut. As for the revived man, he had vanished. Ever since then, that stretch of water has been known to all who sail the lagoon as the Valley of the Seven Dead Men. In reality, the area was already called by this name as early as the 13th century – other records and some 16th-century maps already mention the Valley of the Seven Dead Men. No one knows whether the legend was invented to explain the name of the place, or if the name derives from the story itself, which changes slightly from place to place around the lagoon. Sometimes, for example, there are only six fishermen and the boy, and in some versions, the man pulled from the water is Saint Theodore, who rebukes the fishermen for their wickedness. The tale must have been well known, as even Gabriele D'Annunzio refers to it in the short story *Leda Without the Swan*, writing: 'This table is made from the planks of the boat that fished for seaweed in the Valley of the Seven Dead Men.' The story is still passed down today, by word of mouth and in writing, adding to the air of mystery that lingers over these lagoon waters.

Pink flamingos and sacred ibis

The lagoon is home to a remarkable variety of birdlife. All its natural habitats are protected within areas of community interest, designated as Sites of Community Importance and Special Protection Areas.

The unique landscape of the lagoon – with its expanses of open water, reed beds and rich vegetation – offers an ideal environment for waterbirds, which gather here in large numbers during migration and over the winter.

Numerous species of ducks, geese and swans can be found here,

along with cormorants, egrets, ibises and the spectacular pink flamingos, which in the last decade have become regular visitors, likely due to the establishment of new colonies elsewhere in Italy.
Another notable resident is the sacred ibis, originally from sub-Saharan Africa, easily recognised by its curved bill. It has only recently established itself as a year-round resident.
To appreciate the diversity of birdlife here, it's worth remembering the Venice lagoon is one of the largest wetlands in Europe. It is strictly protected and, to date, an impressive 360 different bird species have been recorded here out of the 550 found across Italy.

CRUCIFIX OF SAN DOMENICO CHURCH ⑮

A work of extraordinary scale

San Domenico Church
Piazza S. Domenico - Chioggia (VE)
Daily 9.30am–12pm and 3pm–5.30pm
Closed Sundays
Bus: line 80 (Venice–Chioggia)
Integrated bus and waterbus transport: line 11 (Lido di Venezia–Pellestrina–Chioggia)

A monumental crucifix standing nearly 5 metres tall – imposing and majestic, impossible to miss – is preserved in San Domenico Church alongside other precious works.

A gnarled Y-shaped cross in fir wood supports a Christ figure carved from poplar, covered with a thin linen cloth painted with natural colours. The effect is profoundly dramatic: the face actually changes expression depending on where you stand. From the left, Christ appears serene in death; from the right, he looks tormented.

The body is roughly carved compared with the carefully detailed face, seemingly recalling the tree of life itself.

At the summit of the cross, an inscription reads *Mors Christi dura monstratur in ista figura* ('the death of Christ is revealed in all its harshness in this image').

Above it sits a pelican, symbolising Christ's sacrifice. Scholars disagree about its origins. Some believe it comes from Strasbourg, pointing to technical tricks typical of areas north of the Alps – like inserting cords into the structure to create three-dimensional wood grain. Others argue it belongs to the Venetian-lagoon tradition, made by an artist familiar with models from the Rhineland.

Several legends surround its origins. According to one, Nicodemus carved it at the foot of the dying Christ with help from angels. The crucifix then travelled from the Holy Land to Jesi in the Marche region, where it miraculously spoke to Saint Peter Martyr.

Legend has it he ordered it to be sent to Venice, but the ship was wrecked off the coast and the crucifix was washed ashore at Chioggia – right where the church stands today.

A different version, recorded in a manuscript by Canon Antonio Boscolo, tells how the crucifix was discovered floating in the water near the Ponte di San Domenico.

Local people carried it to the cathedral, but during the night it mysteriously returned to the spot where they'd found it. The crucifix, it seemed, had chosen its own resting place.

THE WOODEN CART USED TO TRANSPORT THE CHRIST

(16)

A journey into popular devotion to the Christ of San Domenico

Chapel of the Crucifix of San Domenico
San Domenico Church
Piazza S. Domenico - Chioggia (VE)
Daily 9.30am–12pm and 3pm–5.30pm
Closed Sundays (Venezia-Chioggia)
Bus: line 80 (Venice-Chioggia)
Integrated bus and waterbus: line 11 (Lido di Venezia-Pellestrina-Chioggia)

Behind the high altar where the great crucifix stands, is a chapel, maintained by the Arte Popolare group, dedicated to the history and traditions surrounding popular devotion to the Christ of San Domenico.

Here you'll find numerous votive images dedicated to the crucifix, prayers, *tolele* (votive tablets) and the remarkable wooden cart built by engineer Giacomo Schiavuta – once used to carry the Christ through the streets during processions.

For generations, Chioggia's fishermen have held deep veneration for the Christ of San Domenico, painting his image on the hulls and sails of their boats as protection against the dangers of the sea.

The feast of the Christ of San Domenico continues to be celebrated today as it has been since 1500, taking place during Easter week. The procession traditionally winds through the streets carrying a smaller crucifix, making its way to the Palazzo Pretorio, now the town hall.

A procession that ended in bloodshed

The incident known as 'the brawl of the Christ' stands as a dark moment in the procession's history. During the procession on 20 April 1800 (or 25 April, by some accounts), a seemingly trivial accident sparked violence: an Austrian soldier reacted strongly after a boy accidentally bumped into him, likely following the procession. A scuffle broke out between Austrian soldiers and locals who rushed to defend the boy. The situation rapidly deteriorated and firearms were drawn. The final toll proved devastating: 10 dead – seven Chioggia citizens and three Austrian soldiers – with many more wounded on both sides. The authorities banned the procession afterwards, and it remained suspended until 1901, when it was revived with great public celebration.

Between the 18th and 20th centuries, the great crucifix of San Domenico was carried in procession through the city seven times: first in 1745, last in 1965. Some processions became legendary, like the one in 1814, when part of the church facade had to be demolished simply to get the crucifix through the portal. The gimballed cart, now preserved in the chapel, was later devised to tilt the crucifix, allowing it to pass through doorways more easily.

GIUSEPPE OLIVI MUSEUM OF ADRIATIC ZOOLOGY

17

A basking shark in the heart of Chioggia

Palazzo Grassi
Riva Canal Vena 1281
Chioggia (VE)
041 401774
Tuesday, Wednesday and Thursday: 11am–5pm
Friday and Saturday: 7pm–10pm; Sunday: 10am–1pm
Bus: line 80 (Venice–Chioggia)
Integrated bus and waterbus: line 11 (Lido di Venezia–Pellestrina–Chioggia)

At the Giuseppe Olivi Museum of Adriatic Zoology, you can actually touch a basking shark – a female specimen just over 8 metres long that accidentally ended up in fishermen's nets in 2003, about 14 km off the Chioggia coast.

The skin has been preserved through taxidermy, allowing visitors to feel the rough, hard scales that cover a shark's body.

The fascinating marine zoology collection housed in the museum has had quite a journey. It began in the second half of the 19th century in Trieste, where the first marine organisms were collected and studied.

However, when World War I broke out, many researchers were called to arms and the work was disrupted.

After the war ended, the collection was moved to the Italian–German Station in Rovinj, where it was expanded with additional specimens. In 1943, it was transferred to Venice, where it was briefly displayed at the Natural History Museum.

The collection arrived in Chioggia in 1968, though not at its current location – it has only been here since 2010.

Palazzo Grassi itself has an equally complicated history. The building, as you might guess from the name, belonged to the Venetian Grassi family, and the 18th-century structure was designed by Andrea Tiralli. Two plaques at the entrance reveal some of the building's past uses: it first served as a temporary town hall, and then for many years as a hospital.

Restoration took place in the 1990s, and since 2001 the palace has housed Chioggia's cultural activities.

Entrusted to the University of Padua for conservation, the shark has been affectionately nicknamed Olivia by younger visitors.

ST ANDREW TOWER CLOCK

18

The world's oldest tower clock

Corso del Popolo 1318
Chioggia (VE)
Sunday: 10.30am–12.30pm, 5.30pm–6.30pm
Bus: line 80 (Venice–Chioggia)
Integrated bus and waterbus service: line 11 (Venice Lido–Pellestrina–Chioggia)
museocivico@chioggia.org

The tower standing beside St Andrew's church might look like any ordinary bell tower, but it holds an extraordinary surprise. Here, on the fifth floor, you'll find a genuine treasure: the medieval clock mechanism – a work attributed to the Dondi workshop – dating from 1386. According to historical sources, it was already positioned on the north-west tower of the Palazzo Pretorio by that date.

The town council transferred it to the parish of Sant'Andrea in 1839, when the old town hall was demolished and rebuilt.

The clock mechanism consists of two main parts, both in wrought iron: the front section controls the movement of the hand that marks time, while the rear houses the gear train responsible for striking the hours.

The ancient mechanism is separate from the clock face with Roman numerals on the outside of the tower, which runs on a modern electric mechanism.

At its centre is a blue background around which rotates a flaming sun with an extended ray that indicates the hours.

Over the centuries, the clock has undergone repairs and modifications that are still visible today. In 1424, four teeth were replaced on the master wheel, and in the second half of the 18th century a pendulum was added.

St Andrew tower, of Roman–Byzantine origin and standing approximately 30 metres tall, originally served as a lookout point and lighthouse before becoming the church bell tower.

Since 2006, it has housed a museum spread across its seven floors.

Inside you'll find documents, numerous ex-votos, paintings and other objects that bring the city's history to life through faith and popular devotion.

A wonderful view

You can also access the bell chamber, which offers wonderful views over the city of Chioggia and the lagoon.

PAINTING OF PRETE ONSE

19

The ghost of St Andrew's tower

Sant'Andrea Tower Museum
Corso del Popolo 1318 – Chioggia (VE)
Sunday: 10.30am–12.30pm, 5.30pm–6.30pm
Bus: line 80 (Venice–Chioggia)
Integrated bus and waterbus: line 11 (Venice Lido–Pellestrina–Chioggia)
museocivico@chioggia.org

For better or worse, every medieval tower has its ghost, and the tower of St Andrew in Chioggia is no exception.

This particular ghost is rather unusual and even has a nickname: he's called *Prete Onse*, meaning 'the priest who oils', and legend has it that he continues his clockmaker's work throughout the night.

The face you can see in the ceramic painting dedicated to him, displayed in the Sant'Andrea Tower Museum and created in 1969 by artist Luciano Ossetti (1933–2020), is that of Don Vincenzo Veronese, a name recently recovered from the parish archives of Sant'Andrea. From 1876 to 1888, this priest maintained the clock, particularly by regularly oiling the wheels of its mechanism.

In Felice Nordio's *Memorie e ricordi clodiensi 1933–1943* (*Memories and Recollections of Chioggia 1933–1943*), Prete Onse is described as living inside the tower. Due to his difficult temperament, he became something of a hermit: solitary and very serious, he was eventually found dead inside the bell tower itself.

Some maintain that on foggy days, if you look up towards the tower's upper floors, you can still glimpse the light from his lamp.

A lion from the steamship Giudecca?

A parcel arrived one morning in 2023, and inside was a gilded bronze lion – one of those that once adorned the main vessels of A.C.N.I.L., the municipal transport company now known as ACTV. This is what Professor Luciano Bellemo, curator of Chioggia tower, found right outside the entrance. The parcel contained various objects and a note stating that the lion belonged to the steamship Giudecca, which was machine-gunned on 13 October 1944 (see p. 296). While the story's authenticity cannot be confirmed, it carries its own compelling charm. The most touching possibility is that someone, almost 80 years after the tragedy, wanted to return this relic that a family member had probably salvaged from the semi-sunken wreck and treasured for decades. Is this truly the Lion of the Giudecca? Whatever the truth, the small statue has been proudly displayed inside the Sant'Andrea Tower Museum since that day, serving as a reminder of the tragedy that occurred during the last autumn of the war and which left a lasting impact on the Pellestrina and Chioggia communities.

GIORGIO BOSCOLO'S WORKSHOP

20

The shop of the last terracotta pipe maker

Palazzo Granaio
Corso del Popolo
Chioggia
041 4966416
Saturday mornings or by appointment
Bus: line 80 (Venice–Chioggia)
Integrated bus and waterbus: line 11 (Lido di Venezia–Pellestrina–Chioggia)

On the ground floor of Palazzo Granaio, one of the city's oldest buildings, dating from the 14th century, you'll find Giorgio Boscolo's small workshop. Known locally as Femek, he's the last craftsman making traditional terracotta pipes – also called Chioggia pipes – which have always been associated with the town's fishermen.

Made following a process as precise as it is ancient, using clay from the River Po, these pipes are created with a special mould and carefully finished by hand.

To prevent condensation, the bowl (or furnace) has three holes in its base.

The long mouthpiece, or stem, is made from marasca wood – the wild cherry that grows along riverbanks and coastlines – which gives the smoke a distinctive aroma.

Until the mid-17th century, this type of pipe was extremely simple in appearance. Then, around the mid-18th century, glazing and decorative friezes were introduced.

From the second half of the 19th century, pipes were no longer glazed but treated with salt water instead. The craftsmanship of the bowls became particularly refined, and the pipes began to evolve into small sculptures.

Interestingly, during this period one of the most frequently reproduced subjects on the pipes was Queen Victoria's face – apparently out of fondness for the many English artists, especially painters, who were present in Chioggia at that time.

Many used pipes have been found by fishermen on the lagoon floor or in fishing valleys. Others have been discovered on beaches after storms or have emerged from archaeological excavations at the Lazarettos, where smoke was thought to have therapeutic properties.

Still others, particularly factory rejects, have been found on embankments where they were used as landfill material.

Although the advent of cigarettes ended the ancient custom of the terracotta pipe, this tradition has survived thanks to Giorgio Boscolo's dedication.

The craftsman hopes that the Civic Museum of the Southern Lagoon will open a section dedicated to the history and evolution of the Chioggia pipe, so that this tradition won't be completely lost.

WHEELS OF SANTA CATERINA CHURCH

(21)

One of Saint Catherine of Alexandria's principal attributes

Calle S. Caterina, 930 – Chioggia (VE)
September to May: Sunday 5pm–7pm
June, July and August: Sunday 8.30pm–10.30pm
Bus: line 80 (Venice–Chioggia)
Integrated bus and waterbus transport: line 11 (Venice Lido–Pellestrina–Chioggia)

The entrance to Santa Caterina Church opens onto a small square where a large Istrian stone wheel, an 18th-century work by Francesco Venturini, takes centre stage. Look up at the church facade and you'll spot the wheel motif again – in the hands of the saint's statue above the entrance and in the false rose window above it.

This is no coincidence: the wheel is the main iconographic attribute of Saint Catherine of Alexandria and appears throughout the church interior as well.

Renovations carried out over the centuries have altered the church's original appearance. For example, Baldassare Longhena worked here in 1661, and his ornate Baroque style is evident, especially in the 24-metre bell tower.

The richly decorated high altar features an 18th-century altarpiece showing the Glory of Saint Catherine by a Venetian artist. The church has no apse, but look up to see the galleries that frame views of the beautiful upper choir.

There's more to discover: the 18th-century pulpit with its decorative cogwheel is painted in faux marble, while the handsome walnut sacristy from the mid-18th century houses a Crucifixion with Saints from Piazzetta's school. The 1864 organ is one of the last working bellows instruments still in operation.

Climb the staircase to the upper floor, where display cases hold sacred objects and paintings line the walls of Chioggia churches that have since disappeared.

The church's history stretches back to the early 15th century. In 1387, Cistercian nuns from Chioggia and Sottomarina merged their communities in a monastery built east of the Canale Vena on land donated by Pietro Bon.

Thanks to subsequent acquisitions, a large complex developed here. Cistercian nuns lived here until Napoleon suppressed religious orders in 1808. The church then became an outpost of San Giacomo before being entrusted to the Conference of Saint Vincent de Paul in 1860. The diocese bought back the monastery in 1851, giving it to the Canossian Sisters of Charity. Since 2006, no religious sisters have lived here.

MEASURE OF THE FASSO

22

Traces of a commercial past

Piazza XX Settembre - Chioggia (VE)
Bus: line 80 (Venice-Chioggia)
Integrated bus and waterbus transport: line 11 (Lido di Venezia-Pellestrina-Chioggia)

Slightly hidden, carved into the doorpost of the Porta dei Giustizieri near the Fòntego palace and the Loggia dei Bandi in Chioggia, you'll find two vertical lines – one measuring 86 cm, the other 35 cm.

These are the measures of the *fasso*, the standard measurement used by timber merchants.

The word is probably a dialect variation of *passo*, an ancient unit of linear, surface and volume measurement used in Chioggia and throughout the Venetian area (see the guide *Secret Venice* by the same publisher).

The passo wasn't just for lengths – there was also the square passo for calculating land area, and the cubic passo for measuring the volume of materials like stone.

These units were based on local and traditional references, often linked to human body measurements (such as the foot or arm), which explains their geographical variation. Their history is closely tied to the economic and social evolution of the Venetian Republic, which established and controlled these standards to regulate trade and construction.

This measurement system remained in use until the metric system was introduced on 28 July 1861. However, implementation wasn't immediate, and the old local units continued in popular and commercial use for some time.

To help with the transition, the Italian government published comparison tables in 1877, providing exact conversions between the old measurement units of each province (including Venice) and the metric system.

'PARE E FIO': THE TWO BELL TOWERS

23

The oddity of two adjacent structures with completely different stories and sizes

Corso del Popolo – opposite San Giacomo Church
Fondamenta Canal Vena – Chioggia (VE)
Bus: line 80 (Venice–Chioggia)
Integrated bus and waterbus transport: line 11 (Lido di Venezia–Pellestrina–Chioggia)

Only the most observant visitors notice the unusual sight of two bell towers standing just metres apart – or one behind the other – visible from Corso del Popolo, opposite San Giacomo Church, and Fondamenta Canal Vena.

Chioggia residents refer to the bell towers of San Giacomo Church and SS. Trinità as *el pare e el fio* ('father and son') respectively.

Ironically, the 'son' is the older of the two: SS. Trinità. It's also the shorter of the two. Little is known about its structure beyond a 1634 note recording its construction by a certain Giacomo Dei Bei of Chioggia.

What's certain is that it's Chioggia's smallest bell tower.

San Giacomo's tower, by contrast, was built to a design by Aristide Naccari in the late 19th century. At 37.5 metres tall, it almost completely obscures its neighbour.

At the top sits a 2.4-metre weathervane – a rotating angel with trumpet and outstretched wings, similar to one that existed in the ancient sanctuary of Navicella. It dominates the beautiful city, making this tower appear even taller.

CHURCH OF THE HOLY TRINITY AND THE CONFRATERNITY OF THE ROSSI IN CHIOGGIA

24

A little-known gem

Piazza XX Settembre - Chioggia (VE)
September to May: Thursday 9am–noon; Friday, Saturday and Sunday 3pm–5pm
June to August: Thursday 9am–noon; Friday 8.30pm–10.30pm; Sunday 6pm–8pm (June and July only)
Information: 041 405968
Bus: line 80 (Venice–Chioggia)
Integrated bus and boat service: line 11 (Lido di Venice–Pellestrina–Chioggia)

Along the banks of the Canal Vena in the heart of Chioggia stands the Church of the Holy Trinity, a gem that remains relatively unknown.

Step inside and you'll immediately see a beautiful altar depicting the Trinity. Look beyond its columns and you can glimpse the oratory's magnificent coffered ceiling, adorned with precious paintings by various artists including Paolo Piazza, Alvise Benfatti (Veronese's nephew), Palma il Giovane and il Vicentino (Andrea Michieli).

This splendid space was the headquarters of the Confraternity of the Holy Crucifix of the Battuti. The confraternity was officially founded by Capuchin friar Paolo Barbieri and moved between various temporary locations before receiving formal recognition in 1528.

The oratory was once far more lavishly decorated but, during the Napoleonic period, no fewer than 72 paintings were stripped from its walls. Other notable works include two early 17th-century canvases by Pietro Damini and Andrea Michieli at the entrance. They originally hung in the Church of San Nicolò in Chioggia.

In the centre of the church floor lies the tomb of Carlo Moscheni, who served as guardian of the Confraternity from 1703 to 1707 and died on 28 November 1719, though his tombstone mistakenly records 18 November.

Originally built in the 16th century, the church was reconstructed between 1703 and 1707 by architect Andrea Tirali. His design created a Greek cross layout crowned by a central dome. The facade features high reliefs depicting symbols of the Confraternity of the Battuti.

The Confraternity of the Battuti who whipped themselves

The Confraternity of the Holy Crucifix of the Battuti was a penitential congregation of lay flagellants.

During Sunday ceremonies, members whipped their own backs with scourges while reciting litanies.

They wore red habits (hence the alternative name *Rossi*, meaning 'Reds') with openings at the back to allow the flagellation.

Their main charitable works included caring for the sick, sheltering passing pilgrims, providing dowries for girls in need and paying ransoms for prisoners of war.

THE TOLELE OF SAN GIACOMO CHURCH (25)

Votive tablets of prayers and narrow escapes

Corso del Popolo, 1202
Chioggia (VE)
Daily 8.30am–12pm, 4pm–6.30pm
041 400584
Bus: line 80 (Venice–Chioggia)
Integrated bus and waterbus transport: line 11 (Lido di Venezia–Pellestrina–Chioggia)

Inside the presbytery of San Giacomo Church, around 50 *tolele* hang on the walls.

These votive tablets were commissioned mainly by fishermen as tokens of gratitude for answered prayers and lives spared. Similar tablets are also found in other Chioggia churches like San Domenico and the Diocesan Museum, but this is the largest collection.

These tablets are inspired by popular religious devotion, and were created after someone survived a danger or to fulfil a promise. The

person who experienced the miracle would commission a local artist, often one who specialised in these works, to paint their story.

The painters were usually anonymous craftsmen, though some also worked on church frescoes. The quality varies – some are simple folk art, others more refined – depending on who commissioned them: an ordinary fisherman, a wealthy merchant, or even an entire community saved from disaster like fire or plague.

The scenes typically show storms at sea, workplace accidents, domestic mishaps or weapon injuries.

What's fascinating is how the artist combines the moment of danger and the prayer for help in a single image, without worrying about realistic time or space.

The earthly drama unfolds in the lower section while the heavenly intervention appears above, usually separated by painted clouds surrounding divine figures. Most include a caption with the date and the survivor's name.

The tablets are painted on various materials – wood of different qualities, metal like zinc or copper, cardboard, ceramic or glass – using oil, tempera or watercolour.

SHRINE OF THE WITCH'S HOUSE

26

The legend of the cat that escaped through a wall

Ponte Scarpa, 30015 Chioggia VE
Bus: line 80 (Venice–Chioggia)
Integrated bus and waterbus transport: line 11 (Lido di Venezia–Pellestrina–Chioggia)

The 'witch's house', now dilapidated and long for sale, sits at the centre of a mysterious legend.

The story goes that the owners of this dwelling loved going to the theatre. One evening, heading out for a performance, they asked their housekeeper to wait for them.

After finishing her household chores, the woman ate some pumpkin seeds. A cat suddenly appeared before her, having entered from who knows where. Good-naturedly, the woman asked the animal in dialect whether he too would like to eat the *seme* (seeds).

The cat replied *damene, che te farò compagnia* ('give me some, I'll keep you company'). Shocked, she asked the animal whether it was a cat, a soul or the Devil. She grabbed a wooden stick to strike it, but the cat, sensing danger, tried to escape – though the door and windows were shut. So, with its head, it made a hole in the wall and fled. The homeowners are said to have had a shrine built where this happened, depicting the Virgin Mary in half-figure holding the clothed Child on her left.

NEARBY

Garden of San Michele Arcangelo

Station of the State Police
Ramo Padovani, 108 - Chioggia
Monday to Friday 10am–5pm, Saturday 10am–12pm, closed Sunday

In the centre of Chioggia, in a rather hidden spot, there's a charming garden accessed through the entrance corridor of the local police station. It's something you don't expect and which pleasantly surprises visitors. This green space once belonged to the ancient convent of San Francesco dentro le Mura, which housed the Franciscan friars. From the 16th century, Cistercian nuns lived here, carrying out social work such as educating young girls. They gave the place its name – and it's still called *delle muneghette* today.

With Napoleon Bonaparte's arrival, the nuns moved to the Santa Caterina complex and troops took over. Later, the buildings housed a school and various offices, with the western section reserved for the State Police.

MADONNA DEL RIPOSO

27

Where Pope Alexander III paused en route to Venice to sign a peace treaty with Frederick Barbarossa

Bell tower of Santa Maria Assunta Cathedral
Campo del Duomo - Chioggia (VE)
Bus: line 80 (Venice–Chioggia)
Integrated bus and waterbus transport: line 11 (Lido di Venezia–Pellestrina–Chioggia)

Chioggia's tallest structure (56 metres high), the bell tower of Santa Maria Assunta Cathedral, dates from 1347. Above the portal, in a slightly pointed lunette (a semicircular or crescent-shaped decorative space), is a portrayal of the Virgin Mary with the Christ child in her arms. Beside her are Saints Felix and Fortunatus. The work was probably originally polychrome, as suggested by traces of blue visible on the Virgin's crown.

The Madonna is called *del riposo* ('of rest') because legend has it that Pope Alexander III stopped to rest at the foot of this very image while travelling to Venice to sign a peace treaty with Frederick Barbarossa, ending the conflict between the Holy Roman Empire and the Papacy.

To commemorate the event, a lamp hung from the iron bracket – still visible today fixed in the frame – was lit here until the early 20th century. Local tradition held that people would stop beneath it to say a prayer to the Madonna, asking to wake early the following day.

Another place where Pope Alexander III spent the night in Venice

Venice also has a spot where, according to centuries-old tradition, Alexander III stopped to rest: the Calle del Perdon in the San Polo district. Pope Alexander III is said to have slept there, under the Sotoportego de la Madonna (a covered passageway under a building), on the street. Tradition holds that anyone who recites a prayer there will receive plenary indulgence from all sins. See the guide *Secret Venice* by the same publisher.

NEARBY

The bell tower's foundation stone

At the base of the bell tower, bottom left, you can spot the cornerstone laid on 14 November 1347. This stone marks the reconstruction of the tower, which originally dated from the 11th century CE but had collapsed just 10 days before the cornerstone was laid. The inscription is still clearly visible on the stone: + *Rehedificationis* – *Lapis primus* + ('First stone of the rebuilding'). The reconstruction work was completed in 1350.

THE MADONNA DEL SAGRETO OR REFUGIUM PECCATORUM

(28)

A place that inspires great devotion and an unusual ghost story

Bus: line 80 (Venice–Chioggia)
Integrated bus and waterbus: line 11 (Lido di Venezia–Pellestrina–Chioggia)

On the banks of the Canale Perottolo, near the Cathedral of Santa Maria Assunta, there is a "sacred place" where the Refugium Peccatorum stands: a statue of the Virgin Mary with her child, topped by a golden dome. This sculpture was originally located at the top of the Istrian stone loggia that led to the Palazzo Pretorio, demolished in 1837. It is said that those condemned to death would stop in front of this work, commissioned by Podestà Antonio Valmarana but whose author is unknown, for a final prayer.

Located along the shore on an 18th-century balustrade, this sculpture still inspires deep devotion in passers-by today: it is not uncommon to see someone stop there to pray or ask for a favour, just as in the past, when the mothers and wives of fishermen entrusted them to her before they set sail.

Along the balustrade there is also a row of allegorical statues, baskets filled with fruit and a pair of lions bearing coats of arms. One of these statues has no head and is therefore the source of a curious legend.

The legend of the severed head

One of the statues is headless, and this is where a curious legend originates.

It is said that there was a very poor family with five children: one day, one of the girls heard a mysterious voice telling her to cut off the statue's head, because inside she would find a treasure.

She did so and found gold coins inside, which she gave to her parents, improving the family's fortunes.

But whose voice was it that advised her?

It seems to have come from under the cathedral and belonged to someone buried there. It is no surprise that in a seaside town like Chioggia there are legends linked to ghosts!

BALLARIN EXHIBITION AT THE SOUTHERN LAGOON CIVIC MUSEUM 29

Remembering two Chioggia brothers who played for the Grande Torino

Campo Guglielmo Marconi, 1 – Chioggia (VE)
Tuesday to Friday 9am–1pm
Saturday and Sunday 10am–1pm and 2.30pm–6.30pm
Bus: line 80 (Venice–Chioggia)
Integrated bus and waterbus transport: line 11 (Lido di Venezia–Pellestrina–Chioggia)

Opened in October 2021 thanks to the dedication of the nephews and relatives of two celebrated Chioggia brothers who played for the Grande Torino football team, the Ballarin exhibition on the first floor of the Southern Lagoon Civic Museum displays numerous objects that once belonged to them.

A scale model recreates the Basilica of Superga, against whose eastern wall the aircraft carrying the most famous football team of the era crashed on 4 May 1949 – a tragedy that claimed both Ballarin brothers' lives.

This exhibition takes you on a genuine journey through their story and a pivotal moment in Italian history. The Grande Torino represented hope and renewal in post-war Italy, not only for Turin but for the entire nation.

Aldo Ballarin played right-back for the Grande Torino, making 149 appearances, scoring four goals and winning four league titles. He also earned nine caps for the national team.

Dino Ballarin, nicknamed 'the white angel', was understudy to goalkeeper Valerio Bacigalupo and never got the chance to start a match.

The section showing newspapers from the day after the tragedy is particularly moving – a stark reminder of how Italy lost most of its national team players in one terrible moment.

Equally poignant is the extensive collection of photographs from the brothers' funeral in Chioggia on 9 May 1949. Over 40,000 people came to pay their respects and joined the procession to the cemetery.

Beyond Chioggia's stadium, renamed in their honour on 5 March 1950, the Ballarin brothers are also commemorated by stadiums and sports fields in San Benedetto del Tronto (AP), San Felice Circeo (LT), Crespino (RO) and Cercemaggiore (CB), as well as the State Middle School in Valli di Chioggia and a small square in Sottomarina. Aldo Ballarin has an avenue named after him in Rome.

The local football team, Union Clodiense Chioggia SSD, wears maroon as its official colour in tribute to the Grande Torino.

The Ballarin family tomb, where both brothers are buried, can be found in Chioggia cemetery.

The Southern Lagoon Civic Museum also offers a wonderful way to learn more about the city's history. The building stands on the remains of a Franciscan convent from 1314, historically known as *San Francesco fuori le mura* (Saint Francis outside the walls). Damaged during the war between Chioggia and Genoa, it was rebuilt in 1434.

THE MURAZZI OF SOTTOMARINA ㉚

An 18th-century sea defence now surrounded by the town

Via San Marco - Sottomarina
Bus: line 80 (Venice–Chioggia)
Integrated bus and waterbus: line 11 (Lido di Venezia–Pellestrina–Chioggia)

Anyone travelling along Via San Marco in Sottomarina towards Fort San Felice will notice, on the left, the remains of an ancient and imposing structure in Istrian stone.

This construction, roughly 2.6 km long, is what remains of the old *murazzo* (sea wall) built to protect the shore from the power of the sea.

Work began in 1744 following a design by Vincenzo Maria Coronelli and was carried out by Bernardino Zendrini. The project involved building a high wall with an internal core of *pozzolana* (volcanic ash), which was then clad with heavy blocks of Istrian stone.

The sea wall originally ran from Fort San Felice to the Sottomarina Battery, with waves breaking directly against it. Today the situation is completely different – the wall sits surrounded by buildings and streets, with the sea now about a kilometre away.

This change came about through land reclamation – from diverting the River Brenta (1898) and building the harbour breakwaters in the 20th century.

Over the course of the last century, local people demolished parts of the structure to allow urban expansion. In some sections, they lowered the wall by removing the upper portion but kept the base intact. About a hundred metres of the stretch towards Fort San Felice still faithfully shows what the original structure looked like.

The transformations along this part of the coast highlight how dramatically the landscape has changed over the centuries.

It's certainly curious to walk along the line of the sea wall, imagining the sea where buildings, houses, beaches and bathing establishments now stand.

A WALK ALONG THE CA' ROMAN SEA WALL

(31)

Discover an extraordinary structure between the sea and the lagoon

Island of Pellestrina
Open year-round
ACTV bus: line 11

For those who love walking, the Ca' Roman sea wall (*murazzo*) offers one of the most unforgettable routes in the southern lagoon – a walk that should not be overlooked.

Conceived in 1716 by Father Vincenzo Coronelli and built under the supervision of Bernardino Zendrini between 1744 and 1782, this monumental structure was designed to hold back the sea and protect

the barrier islands from erosion.

The most captivating stretch begins near the Pellestrina cemetery and leads you out between the Adriatic Sea and the lagoon, giving the surreal sensation of walking on water.

Walking along the murazzo is a breathtaking experience, but caution is essential – visitors are advised to walk in single file and stay alert, as there are no guardrails or barriers along the way. The destination is just as rewarding. Ca' Roman is a nature reserve, home to coastal woodland and a pristine beach – an ecological gem that has remained almost untouched. The area has been designated a Special Area of Conservation (SAC) and a Special Protection Area (SPA) due to its high environmental value, with more than 200 species of birds having been recorded here.

For history enthusiasts, the landscape is also characterised by the presence of numerous wartime bunkers and a 19th-century fort, now abandoned.

BRONZE BAS-RELIEF COMMEMORATING THE GIUDECCA

32

The Giudecca motor vessel tragedy

Piazzale Ognissanti - Pellestrina (VE)
The shrine is located in the lagoon, in the area facing Piazzale della Chiesa d'Ognissanti
Visible from the shore and accessible by private boat

In Piazzale Ognissanti in Pellestrina, a bronze bas-relief by sculptor Giuseppe Vio commemorates the disastrous sinking of the steamship Giudecca, operated by ACNIL (the Municipal Lagoon Internal Navigation Company), on 13 October 1944.

Every year, during the commemoration, the bas-relief is covered with flowers and laurel wreaths.

The tragedy occurred in the waters facing the Church of Ognissanti.

According to records, the boat departed from Chioggia around 12.30pm on a scheduled service carrying over 200 passengers (almost all civilians, with just a few military personnel). After only 15 minutes at sea, it became the target of three Anglo–American fighter-bombers, which opened fire with machine guns.

The steamship managed to approach Pellestrina, where it was bombed.

Fragments from the vessel reached the settlement of Ognissanti, which was targeted by the fighter-bombers, which continued their assault, spraying the shore with bullets.

As soon as the aircrafts withdrew, local fishermen immediately went to the aid of survivors, first recovering the wounded and then the dead. Officially, there were 67 victims, but it's likely that more people died, as the bodies of some German soldiers were taken away by their comrades and excluded from the final count.

Among those pulled from the lagoon was a little girl who had been thrown into the water. Though she couldn't swim, her wide dress saved her life – the skirt billowed out around her like a life buoy, keeping her afloat long enough for rescuers to reach her.

The tragedy deeply shocked the nation.

Two other commemorative plaques can be found on the cemetery wall. The square in front is dedicated to the memory of those who died on the Giudecca.

Two years after the disaster, a commemorative brass shrine was placed atop a pillar at the exact spot where the accident occurred. Created by Venetian artist Martinuzzi, it features a bronze image of the Madonna and Child. An inscription at the base reads: 'To the victims of the Giudecca / Pellestrina'.

Each year, after a commemorative Mass at the Church of Ognissanti, local authorities travel by boat to lay a laurel wreath at the shrine.

THE 'ALL SAINTS' ALTAR IN THE CHURCH OF OGNISSANTI

33

A truly unusual calendar

Sestiere Busetti - Isola di Pellestrina (VE)
ACTV bus: line 11

Inside the Church of Ognissanti, on the left of the wide nave, stands a very distinctive altar dedicated to 'all saints'. It represents the church's most prestigious treasure: nearly 600 relics from the Holy Land, Egypt, Aquileia, Grado and the dioceses of Malamocco and Chioggia.

The altar functions as a calendar. Display cases are arranged day by day from 1 January to 31 December, each containing the relics of all the saints in the Catholic calendar.

Other sacred remains are kept in reliquaries of various designs, often determined by the size of the bone fragments they contain. These range from pieces several centimetres long in the central part of the altar – where the altarpiece depicting the 'Glory of the Saints' once hung (now positioned above a side door) – to smaller fragments displayed beneath the columns.

At the base of the altar, above the case containing the remains of St Demetria, you'll find relics of St Ursula, St Placidus and St Josephine Bakhita (1869–1947), a Sudanese religious sister who became an Italian citizen and lived for many years in Venice at the Institute of the Catechumens.

Beside the church stands a low bell tower without a spire. Its double windows facing the sea have been walled up to resist the wind from the Adriatic.

Considered the island's cathedral, this church is deeply cherished by the local population. In 1791, Bishop Civran granted it the title of Archpresbyteral. In 1800 it became the seat of the Vicariate of Pellestrina. Since then, the inscription *D.O.M. ARCHIPRESBYTERALE OMNIUM SANCTORUM* has stood prominently on the facade. The Church of Ognissanti is a very old building that has undergone various modifications over the centuries. Its current appearance dates from 1864.

GIORGIO FORESTO'S CASONE

(34)

The floating studio of a highly regarded artist

Opposite Ognissanti Church
Visible from the shore

There's a casone on the lagoon, opposite Ognissanti church, that looks much like any other – perhaps a bit neglected since it's stood empty for years. Nothing about its appearance hints at the remarkable story within, or its connection to Giorgio de Gasperi, considered by some to be the greatest illustrator of the 20th century.

Born near Milan on 30 January 1927, de Gasperi showed exceptional artistic talent from an early age. He studied at Milan's prestigious Brera Academy before building a successful career with major publishing houses, creating many covers for the popular magazine *La Domenica del Corriere*.

Then, at the height of his success – perhaps devastated by his wife's death – he simply disappeared. He retreated to the island of Pellestrina,

where he transformed an old fishing casone, reachable only by boat, into a studio he named *Il mondo della luna*, 'the world of the moon'.

Most islanders never learned his real surname. They called him 'Giorgio Foresto' – *foresto* being the local word for a foreigner, someone from far away or from a different urban and social background.

De Gasperi was intensely private, bartering his remarkable artwork for fruit, vegetables and necessities, keeping interactions with locals to a minimum.

After withdrawing from society, his life became mysterious. What little biographical information exists remains unverified, including tales of him travelling extensively and always returning to his lagoon refuge. Islanders remember him as an eccentric figure who shunned attention and signed all his work simply as Giorgio Foresto.

He died in a Venice care home as he'd lived – alone – on 16 October 2012.

A handful of newspaper articles noted his passing, but his real legacy lives on in countless extraordinary works – some likely still undiscovered, others hanging proudly in Pellestrina homes.

PAINTING OF THE MADONNA OF CARMINE

35

The miracle of the Madonna's moving eyes

Sanctuary of the Madonna dell'Apparizione and Saints Vitus and Modestus
Sestiere Vianelli – Island of Pellestrina (VE)
Bus: line 11

On 4 August 1716, the day Natalino Scarpa encountered a mysterious elderly woman whom the Bishop of Chioggia later determined to have been the Madonna, a series of curious events occurred.

One of these centred on a painting of the Virgin. It originally hung in the sanctuary of Saints Vitus and Modestus, on whose foundations the new church dedicated to the apparition was built, and where we can admire it today.

Chronicles tell us that on that day several women looked through the closed sanctuary door and noticed something astonishing: the Madonna's eyes were moving.

Many people witnessed this phenomenon, and throughout the day pilgrims flocked to see the extraordinary manifestation.

Legend has it that the painting was created on the staves of a barrel by an anonymous traveller as thanks for the hospitality he'd received from a local family.

The image of the Virgin we see today formed part of an altarpiece that originally had the titular saints, Vitus and Modestus, on either side. You can still just make out their hands holding the palms of martyrdom. The Madonna sits against a yellow background with the child on her lap holding a scapular, her gaze turned to the right. Today we admire her on the altar designed by Tiralli, crowned with nine rays. The crown of rays, and the silver moon at her feet, were added in the 19th century.

A work of art examined by Giambattista Tiepolo

The painting attracted the attention of many artists who wanted to examine it, including Giambattista Tiepolo, who believed it to be a work of the Spanish school.

PLAQUE AT THE SANCTUARY OF THE MADONNA DELL'APPARIZIONE

36

Remembering the Virgin's appearance at Pellestrina in 1716 to secure victory over the Ottoman army

Sanctuary of the Madonna dell'Apparizione and Saints Vitus and Modestus
Sestiere Vianelli–Pellestrina (VE)
ACTV bus: line 11

A simple plaque is set into the churchyard in front of the Sanctuary of the Madonna dell'Apparizione.

Blessed by Bishop Monsignor Piasentini in 1966, it reads: 'Here the Blessed Virgin Mary appeared on 4 August 1716 to Natalino Scarpa de Mutti'.

At dawn on 4 August 1716, the Ottoman threat hung over Venice. Near the small church dedicated to Saints Vitus and Modestus, an elderly woman appeared before 14-year-old Natalino Scarpa di Giovanni (known as 'the mute' or, according to other sources, 'dei Mutti').

She wore a black dress adorned with red stars and a white veil over her head. She instructed him to go to the parish priest and ask him to celebrate masses for the souls in Purgatory. Only this, she said, would

secure victory over the Ottoman army.

Natalino went to the priest and relayed the message. The priest listened and did as requested.

Sometime later, Natalino and the other inhabitants of Pellestrina learned that the day after the apparition, the Ottoman army had been defeated at the Battle of Petrovaradin on the Danube.

Thirteen days later, on 18 August, the Turkish fleet suffered a decisive defeat at Corfu.

People immediately understood that the woman Natalino had seen must have been the Virgin Mary. The church was dedicated to her.

Every year on 4 August, the feast of the Madonna dell'Apparizione is celebrated.

The festival is especially cherished by the island's inhabitants and by the wider diocese of Chioggia.

Another miracle

The Sanctuary of the Madonna dell'Apparizione still contains the miraculous painting of the Madonna of Carmine. On that day, 4 August 1716, many witnesses saw its eyes move (see previous double page).

NEARBY

The plaque on Natalino Scarpa's house

A plaque on Natalino Scarpa's house marks his birth on 25 December 1701 and commemorates the Virgin's appearance at Pellestrina on 4 August 1716. After the miraculous event, the young man from Pellestrina entered the priesthood. The Senate funded his studies at the Seminary of San Cipriano in Murano, and he was ordained on 26 May 1725 by the Bishop of Torcello. In 1735 he became Rector of the Pellestrina Sanctuary alongside Don Domenico Busetto. He died on 31 October 1776 and was buried in the Church of Ognissanti.

PLAQUE COMMEMORATING THE SHIP KADIMA

37

Remembering the journey of 794 Jewish migrants bound for Palestine in 1947

Strada comunale della Laguna
Zona Piovini, Sestiere Scarpa - Isola di Pellestrina (VE)
Autobus ACTV: linea 11

'From this shore on 5 November 1947, the ship Kadima set sail with 794 Jewish migrants bound for Palestine.'

These words are inscribed on a plaque in the Piovini area of Pellestrina, within the Sestiere Scarpa, commemorating an event in which this long, narrow island between sea and lagoon played a key role.

Although little known outside the local area, it is a story that deserves to be remembered.

Between 1945 and 1948, more than 25,000 Jews passed through Italy after the racial persecutions, embarking for Palestine.

Three ships set sail from Pellestrina, carrying a total of 1,305 Jewish people who had survived the extermination camps of Eastern Europe.

The ship to which the plaque is dedicated was originally named Raffaelluccia (in some texts it is referred to as Rafael Luccia), but for this particular voyage it was renamed *Kadima* – Hebrew for 'Forward'.

After departing from Pellestrina, the ship was intercepted by the British and diverted to Haifa. The United Kingdom had prohibited Jewish immigration to Palestine from 1933 until 1948 to avoid upsetting the numerical balance between Jews and Arabs in the area.

From Haifa, the passengers were transferred to another ship and taken to a British internment camp in Cyprus. From there, in January 1948, they were finally able to reach their destination.

The plaque commemorating Kadima was installed in 2017 through the initiative of Venice's Jewish community and the municipalities of Lido and Pellestrina.

> Aliyah Bet is the codename used between 1920 and 1948 for the clandestine immigration of Jews to territories under the British Mandate in Palestine.

THE 1966 WAVE MEMORIAL (38)

A monument in memory of the day Pellestrina nearly disappeared

Strada della Laguna, Portosecco
ACTV bus: line 11

It's a simple yet powerful monument: a wave carved in stone in 1967, just one year after the date inscribed below it – 4 November 1966.

It was created to pass on the memory of the day when Pellestrina came close to vanishing forever, so that future generations would not forget.

Visiting this sculpture is an invitation to pause and reflect on an extraordinary event that brought the island to its knees. And yet, despite the fear, the people of Pellestrina emerged more united than ever, ready to rebuild and start again.

Friday, 4 November 1966 is an unforgettable date in the history of the Venetian Lagoon, etched into the memories of everyone who lived through that endless day.

That was when Venice and its islands were hit by an exceptional weather event – a tidal surge unlike anything seen before.

Several factors converged to bring the lagoon to the brink: it had been raining for days, and major rivers like the Piave, Tagliamento and Adige were all in flood, further raising the water level. To make matters worse, a strong sirocco wind and low atmospheric pressure intensified the storm surges in the Adriatic Sea.

The regular tide couldn't drain away before the next one arrived, driven relentlessly by the warm wind, piling one high tide on top of the first one which occurred on the evening of 3 November.

By the next morning, the sea had broken through the murazzi (the island's historic sea walls) in three places, flooding into the lagoon and submerging the entire island.

Residents were evacuated using boats provided by ACNIL (the City's Internal Lagoon Navigation Service) and taken to the Ospedale al Mare on the Lido of Venice.

As the hours passed, weather conditions seemed to be worsening still, but then, as suddenly as it arrived, the sirocco died down, replaced by a *libeccio* (south-westerly) wind.

It took many hours for the water to recede, and the days that followed were just as harsh. The damage was immense and ran into staggering figures.

The stories of those who lived through it are deeply moving, and the photos and video footage from the time are equally striking – especially the images captured by Duilio Stigher, an RAI news cameraman whose extraordinary footage of Venice aired on the evening news that very day.

LITTLE MUSEUM OF THE SOUTHERN LAGOON

(39)

A hidden gem of local culture you won't want to miss

Former Carlo Goldoni Primary School
San Pietro in Volta, Pellestrina
info@museopellestrina.it
museopellestrina.it
ACTV bus: line 11

Inaugurated in 2007, the Little Museum of the Southern Lagoon is a charming local treasure that's absolutely worth a visit. Housed in the former Carlo Goldoni Primary School, it offers an engaging experience for visitors of all ages. Its four rooms are full of surprises and offer unique, illuminating perspectives on the southern lagoon's most important features.

The museum is run entirely by volunteers, and its main goal is to protect and promote the history of the island of Pellestrina.

The visit begins on the ground floor in the White Room, which focuses on the island and its sea defences, supported by scale models and explanatory panels that guide visitors through the topic.

The Black Room is dedicated to *l'Acqua Granda*, the big flood of 1966 that struck the island.

It is told through photographs and a video produced by the City of Venice in 1996, 30 years after the disaster, featuring original testimonies and documents.

Upstairs, the Blue Room is dedicated to lagoon and sea fishing. Beautifully detailed models show the seabed teeming with *cogoli*, *chebe*, and traditional fishing boats gliding along.

The walls are lined with traditional tools and reproductions of local fish species.

Finally, inaugurated in February 2025, there is a room dedicated to boatyards, *squeri*, and lagoon and sea vessels. This space features numerous model boats, reproductions of traditional boatyards, and a collection of original tools once used on board.

The museum's historical materials and documents have been gathered through years of research, with some items donated by the associations *El Fughero* and *Abitanti in Isola*.

The museum continues its cultural work online as well, with a website offering digital documents and free resources, including university theses focused on the island.

LA PALATA DELLE CEPPE

(40)

The last of the guardian piers built after 1500 to control shifting sands

A small breakwater near the Santa Maria del Mare landing point – visible from land and from the ferry that connects the Lido of Venice to Pellestrina (line 11)

You'll pass it on the five-minute ferry ride between the Lido of Venice and the island of Pellestrina – a route also used by large vessels heading to the commercial port of Marghera or out toward the open sea.

This is the Palata delle Ceppe, a low, broken stretch of reef – once part of a defensive structure. It's the last remaining example of the *palade* or guardian piers (also known as *speroni* or breakwaters), built shortly after 1500 at the mouth of the Malamocco port inlet. Their purpose was to redirect the flow of sand and deposit it on the shoreline, helping to maintain clear navigable routes for ships bound for Poveglia and San Marco.

The other piers that once stood at the southern tip of the Alberoni have since disappeared, been buried or absorbed into the vast sandy stretch created by the construction of the northern breakwater between 1836 and 1845.

Built atop the Palata delle Ceppe are a fishing platform and a small red-light beacon known as the Faro delle Ceppe. Built in 1912, this 10-metre-high candelabra-style lighthouse is mounted on a red base and is the only lighthouse from the old navigation light system still in operation.

The deepest point in the northern Adriatic

Not far from this modest reef lies a trench that plunges down to 50 metres below sea level – the deepest point in the northern Adriatic. It was created by powerful currents that formed after the opening of the Canale dei Petroli in 1969.

Local fishermen say that many fishing nets and bits of debris were deliberately sunk there over the years. Because of that – and the strong, unpredictable currents that are always present – diving in this area is strongly discouraged.

It was September 1995 and Thomas Jonglez was in Peshawar, the northern Pakistani city 20 kilometres from the tribal zone he was to visit a few days later. It occurred to him that he should record the hidden aspects of his native city, Paris, which he knew so well. During his seven-month trip back home from Beijing, the areas he crossed took in Tibet (entering clandestinely, hidden under blankets in an overnight bus), Iran and Kurdistan. He never took a plane but travelled by boat, train or bus, hitchhiking, cycling, on horseback or on foot, reaching Paris just in time to celebrate Christmas with the family.

On his return, he spent two fantastic years wandering the streets of the capital to gather material for his first 'secret guide', written with a friend. For the next seven years he worked in the steel industry until the passion for discovery overtook him. He launched Jonglez Publishing in 2003 and moved to Venice three years later.

In 2013, in search of new adventures, the family left Venice and spent six months travelling to Brazil, via North Korea, Micronesia, the Solomon Islands, Easter Island, Peru and Bolivia.

After seven years in Rio de Janeiro, he now lives in Berlin with his wife and three children.

Jonglez Publishing produces a range of titles in nine languages, released in 40 countries.

FROM THE SAME PUBLISHER

ATLASES OF CURIOSITIES

Atlas of abandoned France
Atlas of extreme weather
Atlas of forbidden places
Atlas of geographical curiosities
Atlas of geographical curiosities – Britain
Atlas of unusual wines

PHOTO BOOKS

Abandoned America: The Age of Consequences
Abandoned Asylums
Abandoned Australia
Abandoned Belgium
Abandoned Churches: Unclaimed Places of Worship
Abandoned Cinemas of the World
Abandoned France
Abandoned Germany
Abandoned Lebanon
Abandoned Italy
Abandoned Japan
Abandoned Spain
Abandoned USSR
Abandoned World – An AI-generated exploration
After the Final Curtain: The Fall of the American Movie Theater
After the Final Curtain: America's Abandoned Theaters
Baikonur – Vestiges of the Soviet Space Program
Cinemas – A French Heritage
Chernobyl's Atomic Legacy – 25 years after disaster
Clickbait – A visual journey through AI-generated stories
Destination: Wellness – Our 35 best places in the world to take time out
Forbidden Places – Exploring our Abandoned Heritage
Forbidden France
Forgotten Heritage
Oblivion
Secret Sacred Sites
The cinemas of India – An exceptional heritage
Unusual Hotels – World
Venice deserted
Venise from the skies

'SOUL OF' GUIDES

Soul of Amsterdam - A guide to the 30 best experiences
Soul of Athens - 30 experiences
Soul of Barcelona - 30 experiences
Soul of Berlin - A guide to the 30 best experiences
Soul of Brussels - A guide to exceptional experiences
Soul of Detroit - A guide to exceptional experiences
Soul of Kyoto - A guide to exceptional experiences
Soul of Lisbon - A guide to exceptional experiences
Soul of Los Angeles - A guide to exceptional experiences
Soul of Marrakesh - A guide to exceptional experiences
Soul of Marseille - A guide to exceptional experiences
Soul of Milan - A guide to exceptional experiences
Soul of New York - A guide to 30 exceptional experiences
Soul of Paris - 30 experiences
Soul of Rome - A guide to exceptional experiences
Soul of Tokyo - A guide to exceptional experiences
Soul of Venice - A guide to exceptional experiences
Soul of Vienna - A guide to exceptional experiences

SECRET ATLASES

London – The secret atlas
New York – The secret atlas
Paris – The secret atlas
Venice – The secret atlas

'SECRET' GUIDES

Secret Amsterdam
Secret Bali – An unusual guide
Secret Bangkok
Secret Barcelona
Secret Bath – An unusual guide
Secret Belfast
Secret Berlin
Secret Boston – An unusual guide
Secret Brighton – An unusual guide
Secret Brooklyn – An unusual guide
Secret Brussels
Secret Budapest
Secret Buenos Aires
Secret Campania
Secret Cape Town
Secret Copenhagen
Secret Dolomites
Secret Dublin – An unusual guide
Secret Edinburgh – An unusual guide
Secret Florence
Secret French Riviera
Secret Geneva
Secret Glasgow – An unusual guide
Secret Granada
Secret Helsinki
Secret Istanbul
Secret Johannesburg
Secret Kuala Lumpur
Secret Lisbon
Secret Liverpool – An unusual guide
Secret London – An unusual guide
Secret London – Unusual bars & restaurants
Secret Los Angeles – An unusual guide
Secret Louisiana – An unusual guide
Secret Madrid
Secret Mexico City
Secret Milan
Secret Montreal – An unusual guide
Secret Naples
Secret New Orleans – An unusual guide
Secret New York – An unusual guide
Secret New York – Curious activities
Secret New York – Hidden bars & restaurant
Secret Normandy
Secret Paris
Secret Potsdam
Secret Prague
Secret Provence
Secret Rio de Janeiro
Secret Rome
Secret Seville
Secret Singapore
Secret Strasbourg
Secret Sussex – An unusual guide
Secret Tokyo
Secret Tuscany
Secret Venice
Secret Washington D.C. – An unusual guide
Secret York – An unusual guide

Follow us on Facebook and Instagram

Albanese G., Borghi M., Memoria resistente. La lotta partigiana a Venezia e provincia nel ricordo dei protagonisti, uovadimensione, Portogruaro (VE) 2005.

Armani E., Caniato G., Cianola R., I cento cippi di conterminazione lagunare, Istituto Veneto di Scienze, Lettere ed rti, Venise 1991.

Baldan L., Giulini P., Monetti P., 'Tecnica costruttiva del casone' in Natura e ambiente in Saccisica e dintorni, Banca di redito Cooperativo di Piove di Sacco, 2005.

Bertelli S., Pietre d'inciampo. Cinque itinerari della memoria a Venezia (1943 – 1945), nuovadimensione, Portogruaro VE) 2023.

Bertoldi F., Paladin A. (2012), 'Le mummie egizie conservate nelle collezioni museali veneziane' in Zanovello P., iampini E.M.(dir.), Frammenti d'Egitto: Progetti di catalogazione, provenienza, studio e valorizzazione delle antichità gizie ed egittizzanti - Actes de colloque (Padoue, 15-16 novembre 2010), CLEUP, Padoue 2010.

Bozzato G., Costantini R., Santostefano P., Trevisan V., Vian A., Edifici storici del litorale del Cavallino, tipografia ardin, Treporti (VE) 1996.

Caloi P., 'I casoni : colpo di fantasia o eredità culturale ?' in Etnie - Scienza Politica e Cultura dei popoli minoritari N.8, 984.

Cappai C., Segantini M.A., Infrastrutture dello sguardo. Il restauro della Torre Massimiliana nell'isola di Sant'Erasmo Venezia, Marsilio, Venise 2004.

Cappellini P., Le Polveriere Venete, Editrice Cesare Ferrari di Clusone, Bergame 1987.

Carraro M, L'isola di San Clemente a Venezia. Storia, restauro e nuove funzioni, Carsa Edizioni, Pescara 2005.

Cattabiani A., Santi d'Italia. Vita, leggende, iconografia, feste, patronati, culto, Rizzoli, Milan 2018.

Cortelazzo M., 'Una leggenda dei pescatori veneti in periodical Lares Vol. XXVIII N. 3/4 (July–December) 1962), pp. 22-128, Olschki Editore, Florence 1962.

Cortellazzo M., Religiosità popolare – Le tavolette votive, Amilcare Pizzi Editore per Cassa di Risparmio di Padova e ovigo, coll. Cultura Popolare del Veneto, 1992.

Costantini S., Molin M., 'I Santi Patroni di Burano : un complicato enigma nell'agiografia medievale' in Quaderni orcellani n.6, Centro Studi Torcellani 2013.

Crovato G., Tagliapietra M., Vianello R., Pellestrina, Il Poligrafo, 2020.

Cuchetti C.A., Padovan A., Seno S., La storia documentata del Litorale Nord, Editrice Armena, Venise 1976.

De Francovich G., 'L'origine e la diffusione del crocifisso gotico doloroso' in Römisches Jahrbuch für Kunstgeschichte, p.145-261, 1938.

Eleuteri P., Fiaccadori G., Brusegan M., San Michele in Isola. Isola della conoscenza, ottocento anni di storia e cultura amaldolesi nella laguna di Venezia, Catalogo, Utet, 2012.

Francescutti E., Crocifissi lignei a Venezia e nei territori della Serenissima 1350-1500. Modelli diffusione restauro, entro Studi Antoniani, Padoue 2013.

Gerolamo F. (dir.), Venezia : isola del Lazzaretto Nuovo, Guides archéologiques de la lagune de Venise, Archeoclub 'Italia, Venise 2004.

Gusson Spadari R., 'La centenaria storia dell'Oratorio di San Domenico', article published in the local press.

Gusson Spadari R., 'La Madonnina ritrovata', article published in the local press.

'L'Idrovora di Lova', Quaderno n.1, Consorzio di Bonifica Acque Risorgive, février 2024.

Longhin E., Le valli della laguna di Venezia : da pubblico demanio a privato dominio?, Province de Venise, Venise 2004.

Malagnini F., Il Lazzaretto Nuovo di Venezia. Le scritture parietali, Franco Cesati Editore, Florence 2017.

Malagnini F., Il Lazzaretto Vecchio di Venezia. Le scritture epigrafiche, Marcianum Press, Venise 2018.

Manfrin M., 'La sosta al Moranzan', essay published in Rive : uomini, arte, natura n. 9, 2013.

Marangon G., Antiche simbologie nel cuore religioso di Chioggia, Edizioni Nuova Scintilla, 2006.

Marangon G., Chiesa e comunità monastica di Santa Caterina in Chioggia, Edizioni Nuova Scintilla, 2019.

Marangon G., Chiese storiche del Litorale, Edizioni Nuova Scintilla, 2012.

Marangon G., Chiese storiche di Chioggia, co-published by the Diocese of Chioggia et Edizioni Nuova Scintilla, 2011.

Marangon G., Chiostri e cori monastici di Chioggia, Edizioni Nuova Scintilla, 2015.

Marchesi P., Il forte di Sant'Andrea a Venezia, Stamperia di Venezia Editrice, 1978.

Marco Toso Borella, I dossali di San Zuanne, Associazione culturale L'isola Invisibile, Venise 2009.

Moine C., Chiostri tra le acque. I monasteri femminili della laguna nord di Venezia nel basso Medioevo, All'Insegna el Giglio, 2013.

Molin M., 'La chiesa di Santa Caterina di Mazzorbo. Autentico gioiello lagunare' in Quaderni Torcellani n. 3, Centro tudi Torcellani, Venise 2010.

Molin M., 'Santa Barbara di Nicomedia. Storia, leggenda e devozione dall'Oriente a Burano' in Quaderni Torcellani n. , Centro Studi Torcellani, 2011.

Molin M., 'O Beata Solitudo...O Sola Beatitudo. Breve storia dell'isola di San Francesco del Deserto' in Quaderni orcellani n. 7, Centro Studi Torcellani, 2020.

Moschini G.A., Guida per la città di Venezia all'amico di Belle Arti, vol. II, p. 447, Venise, 1815.

Museo Archeologico Nazionale di Altino – Guide thématique.

Nebbia U., 'Una dimora di caccia e pesca nell'isoletta di Valle Zappa nella Laguna di Venezia' in Architettura e arti ecorative, instalment XII, p. 566, août 1930.

Padoan A., Almanacco di Chioggia, vol. 6, Edizioni Nuova Scintilla, Chioggia 2006.

Pampagnin V., Il coraggio di scegliere. Resistenza e resistenti : riflessioni e approfondimenti, Centro studi Ettore uccini, 2010.

Pellizzer L., Da San Martino di Campalto a Terzo di Tessera. Il territorio della gronda lagunare di Venezia nei ocumenti della Mensa Patriarcale, 2022.

Peron P., Luoghi del culto popolare lungo la Riviera del Brenta, Fiesso d'Artico (VE), Grafiche La Press on behalf of otary Club Venezia-Riviera del Brenta, Venise 1996.

Polo G., Berati P., Polo G., 'Mira ricorda la lapidaria nel territorio' in Rive, uomini, arte, natura n. 4, 2004.

Rallo G., 'La Valle Millecampi. Il sito ambientale e naturalistico – L'oasi naturalistica "Valle Averto"', appendix in La alle Millecampi, Province de Padoue - Etudes sur le territoire, l'environnement et le paysage, 1995.

Riva E., 'L'Antica farmacia di San Servolo a Venezia' dans Atti e memorie, quarterly publication of l'A.I.S.F., 1996.

Rocco L., Vie di terra, d'acqua, di ferro e d'aria. Racconti e immagini di Camponogara, Coop. Il Plaustro, Prozzolo 2009.

Santostefano P., L'isola della Chiesa a Treporti. Storia di un borgo rurale nella laguna nord di Venezia (sec. XVI-XX), enise 2002.

Santostefano P., Arte e fede nelle isole treportine, grafiche Nardin, 2007.

Santostefano P., Le Porte del Cavallino, storie di imprenditori, commerci e osterie, Tipolitografia Biennegrafica, 2022.

Scroccaro M., I forti di Venezia, Mattioli 1985, 2015.

Signore G.G., Apostolatus Maris – MARIPORT – Breve storia della Fondazione S. Maria del Porto (1953-1996), rafiche Tre snc, 1997.

SIUSA Archivi Storici della Chiesa di Venezia.

• Stringa N., Scotton F., Rossi G., Lettere e scritti dispersi, Canova 2021.
• Torricelli P., Bon M., Mizzan L., 'Aspetti naturalistici della laguna e laguna come risorsa', research report 03.97 in Part Prima: Aspetti naturalistici della laguna, Istituto Veneto di Scienze, lettere ed Arti, Venise 1997.
• Tosello V., L'isola della Madonna dell'Apparizione, arcipretale di Ognissanti (éd.), Pellestrina 1991.
• Turri E., Caniato G., Zanetti M., La laguna di Venezia, Cierre Edizioni, 2008.
• Valli Veneziane, natura storia e tradizioni delle Valli da pesca a Venezia e Caorle, Province de Venise, département de l chasse, de la pêche et de la police nationale (dir.), Cicero Editore, Venise 2009.
• Vanzan Marchini N.-E. (dir.), Rotte mediterranee e baluardi di sanità. Venezia e i lazzaretti mediterranei, Skira Milan 2004.
• Zangirolami C., Storia delle chiese, dei monasteri, delle scuole di Venezia rapinate e distrutte da Napoleone Bonaparte Arti Grafiche E. Zanelli, Mestre 1962.
• Zecchin F. (dir.), La valle Millecampi, La Garangola, Padoue 1994.
• Zorzi A., Venezia Scomparsa, Arnoldo Mondadori Editore, Milan 2001.

THANKS TO:

Alessandro Scarpa Marta, for always enthusiastically supporting our research work, for his passion for heritage and for his willingness to introduce us to friendly people and extraordinary aspects of the island of Pellestrina.

Giorgio Bonaldo, Marco Farnea, and Maurizio Gusson, for their willingness to accompany us in their boat during the phase of collecting photographic material in the northern lagoon and in the valleys of the southern lagoon.

The religious community of the brothers of San Francesco del Deserto, for the hospitality and courtesy they showed us during our visit to the island.

Giacomo Dalla Pietà for his valuable advice in translating the Latin inscription on Forte Sant'Andrea relating to Venice's victory at Lepanto.

SPECIAL THANKS TO:

Luca Azzano Cantarutti, Angelica Baslini, Renzo Battaglia, Luciano Bellemo, Gilberto Bertoncello, Giada Bonigolo, Gianni Bonigolo, Alessia Boscolo Nata, Pietro Calza, Cristiano Capponi, Alessandra Crocco Giacomo Dalla Pietà, Maurizio Eltri, Fiorella "Cosetta " Enzo, Andrea Falconi, Ferruccio Falconi, Rossella Favero, Gianni Fazzini, Rudy Ferro, Giorgio Gorin, Renata Gusson, Inna Konovalenko, Aldo Izzo, Manuela Moro, Mario Nason, Giorgio Malavasi, Stefania Montagner, Manuel Paganuzzi, Lorenza Palma, Federica Pancin, Lionello Pellizzer, Alberto Peratoner, Nicoletta Piccoli Emmer, Dino Pistolato, Melania Pregnolato Alessandra Previtali, Sonia Reginato, Giorgio Scarpa, Rino Sgarbossa, Thusitha Solangaachchi, Michael Sorgato, Artemio Tagliapietra, Vittorio Talvacchia, Matteo Tassetto, Giovanni Valdo, Alessandra Vedovato Piero Vianello, Francesco Vidal, Daniela Zanella, Mirco Zanotto, Daniela Zamperetti, Fabrizia Zamarchi Cesarino Zanusso, Federico Zubiolo.

Thanks also to: Associazione Abitanti in Isola, Associazione Terra Antica, Consorzio di Bonifica Acque Risorgive, Corporazione Piloti dell'Estuario Veneto and to all the people, organizations, and associations who made themselves available.

Cartography: **Cyrille Suss** – Layout: **Emmanuelle Willard Toulemonde** – Translation: **Olivia Fuller** – Copy editing: **Lee Dickinson** – Proofreading: **Abigail Kafka** – Publishing: **Clémence Mathé**

Registration of copyright: January 2026 – Edition: 01
ISBN: 978-2-36195-878-7
Printed in Bulgaria by Dedrax